Business Process Reengineering

Business Process Reengineering

Breakpoint Strategies for Market Dominance

HENRY J. JOHANSSON
PATRICK McHUGH
A. JOHN PENDLEBURY
WILLIAM A. WHEELER III

JOHN WILEY & SONS
Chichester · New York · Brisbane · Toronto · Singapore

Published 1993 by John Wiley & Sons Ltd
Baffins Lane, Chichester
West Sussex PO19 1UD, England

Reprinted August and November 1993, March 1994

First published in paperback July 1994

Other Wiley Editorial Offices

John Wiley & Sons, Inc., 605 Third Avenue,
New York, NY 10158-0012, USA

Jacaranda Wiley Ltd, 33 Park Road, Milton,
Queensland 4064, Australia

John Wiley & Sons (Canada) Ltd, 22 Worcester Road,
Rexdale, Ontario M9W 1L1, Canada

John Wiley & Sons (SEA) Pte Ltd, 37 Jalan Pemimpin #05-04,
Block B, Union Industrial Building, Singapore 2057

Library of Congress Cataloging-in-Publication Data

Business process reengineering : breakpoint strategies for market
  dominance / Henry J. Johansson . . . [et al.].
      p.   cm.
    Includes index.
    ISBN 0-471-93883-1
    1. Total quality management.   2. Just-in-time systems.
  3. Industrial management.   I. Johansson, Henry J.
  HD62.15.B87   1993
  658.5'62—dc20   93–7341
                                                            CIP

British Library Cataloguing in Publication Data

A catalogue record for this book is available from the British Library

ISBN 0-471-93883-1 (cloth)

ISBN 0-471-95088-2 (paper)

Typeset in 11/13pt Palatino by
Mathematical Composition Setters Ltd, Salisbury, Wiltshire
Printed and bound in Great Britain by
Biddles Ltd, Guildford and King's Lynn

We dedicate this effort to our wives:
Helene, Henrietta, Juliet and Meg
with love and sincere thanks

Contents

Preface

For the past 15 years we have been supporting our clients' efforts to implement operational improvement programs. These programs have gone under headings such as Manufacturing Resource Planning (MRP II) and Total Quality Management (TQM). We have advanced our knowledge and applied new concepts in areas such as strategic planning and in the implementation of change. Much of this work has been functionally based and we have supported improvements as diverse as distribution networks and new product design teams. We have worked with clients in the application of advanced technologies such as robotics, automation and computer-aided design and manufacturing. In the great majority of cases our clients have been extremely pleased with the results that were achieved. Breakthroughs literally became commonplace; lead times and, thus, inventories were reduced by as much as 90 percent, productivity improvements were astounding when compared to earlier tactical efforts, cost of quality was reduced by orders of magnitude, and, most importantly, everyone felt the pride of contributing to a substantial improvement in performance. As coaches and consultants we had earned "brownie points" back in the office. We were helping many businesses and thought that we must be at or near the top of the heap in our chosen profession.

While feeling good about past achievements, however, we slowly came to realize that we had not served the client completely. Companies had achieved new levels of operational excellence, but in the majority of instances the improvements were not leveraged throughout the entire organization or the marketplace. It was great to improve manufacturing, engineering and distribution businesses or the back room operations in service industries, but the improvements were usually transparent to the market. Business strategists continued to develop market strategies that identified what products would be sold, to whom they would be sold, and where they would be sold. Rarely, if ever, did their strategy consider operational excellence as a basis for competitive dominance. In other words, strategies missed out on *how* a company would compete. This book then is *our* attempt to right the years of strategic omission with our explanation of *how* to achieve strategic breakthroughs.

About six years ago two of us were part of an internal task force within our international organization that tried to develop an approach to business strategy that would leverage operational excellence into the marketplace. For a year or so it was a fruitless effort. The strategy-oriented members of the team talked in grand concepts while we, with an operations bent, kept trying to "translate" the concepts into pragmatic methodologies and technologies. We could not get them down from 40 000 feet while we, in turn, were struggling to get off the runway.

Then we picked up on the consequences of thinking through the broad business implications by applying Michael Hammer's notions of Business Process Reengineering (BPR). We saw that it had the potential to be as revolutionary as JIT was when it was first introduced into the Western world in 1978. While JIT attacked the foundations of functional Taylorism and taught us to think of continuous flow synchronized to real demand, BPR gave us the wherewithal to think of a defunctionalized organization that always focused on the customer or the customer's customer. We finally had the mechanism to create strong synergy between market strategy and operations. As one colleague commented, "Finally the clouds have hit the ground."

When all of us first started in consulting (with 72 years of aggregate experience since), the assignments were discrete in nature: improve inventory accuracy, implement a piece-work system, lay out a distribution center, etc. With the arrival of the

JIT philosophy in 1978 we could begin to look at ways of managing with speed and quality. We could begin to leverage our industrial engineers, quality statisticians, materials managers, purchasing experts and designers toward a common goal. But, for the most part we made the mistake of keeping up the functional barriers. We set up Quality Teams who were empowered to create and effect new ways of working within their specific area or function. Management continued to manage the numbers, but change was occurring; it vigorously supported the continuous improvement efforts on the shop-floor or in the back office. With the advent of Business Process Reengineering (BPR) a new way of managing is emerging. Processes are managed, not functions. Management keeps its eye on the "new assets," not the "old" ones. Top management's new role is to manage the angst of being proactive and radical, the Zeitgeist that is required in the new marketplace. Global competition has forced management to re-evaluate the way multinational operations and markets operate as the power of the big corporations has been challenged, most notably by the lean and nimble. The not-so-old idea of continuous improvement needs to be re-addressed. Operational strategies are driving business strategies. Compared to when we first started in industry and then consulting, *it is a whole new business world in which we work*. And it is more fun than ever!

Throughout this book we use the phrase "break the china." Like any good business phrase, "paradigm breaking" has been over-used and is beginning to mean something different to each advocate. Therefore, we have chosen to use the phrase break the china as a means of conceptualizing a whole new beginning for a business. We do not just mean challenging the way a particular task or activity is performed; we ask the reader to step back and challenge the very business that they are in and question what should be the real basis of competition. Just as formal china sets are passed from generation to generation, so are ideas and ways of working. While we are not advocating that the reader rushes to the cupboard and smashes great-grandmother's Staffordshire, we are proposing that every concept, assumption, purpose, and principle is temporarily abandoned so that totally new ways are considered. As

Chapter 4 suggests, there are ways of putting the china back together such that the best of traditions and technologies are retained, but a whole new "pattern" emerges in great-grandmother's china.

The reader may wonder why two Englishmen and two Americans collaborated to write this book. In the past, new concepts or approaches tend to gain acceptance in different time periods within each region. BPR seems to break this norm. There is a realization that no matter where a business is located or headquartered, the necessity for a step change in perform-ance will be a prerequisite for leapfrogging the competition. Each of us spends a considerable amount of time consulting in each other's country. BPR has become a totally common denominator in our transnational consulting. As Chapter 7 indicates, the approach we describe is a prerequisite for effec-tive globalization. For these reasons, it seemed only natural that we should write this book together, aiming to create a global perspective. Added to that, we each have a profound respect for each other's ideas and experience.

Lest the reader think that there is total commonality between our countries of origin, it should be noted that some interesting cultural differences did appear. Ranging from the British total aversion to dangling particles to the American penchant for inventing words, we have had some heated discussions. We each gave and took. An example is the word "virtuality" that appears throughout the book. One of us was aghast at the word since it is not in the dictionary (Oxford) and therefore "no self-respecting Englishman would employ such a word." An American job shop is called a one off factory. We considered including a glossary of terms (English to American and vice versa), but it may have ended up longer than the text itself. In the true ecumenical spirit, the book uses American English and was printed in England (much to the consternation of the English copy editor). We are nevertheless united in the concepts presented in this book.

There were many individuals who have influenced our thoughts during the preparation of this book, and we owe them a debt of gratitude for sharing their ideas with us. The ideas of Giorgio Merli, a colleague from Italy, fueled the intro-duction for Chapter 1. Bill Band, from Canada, taught us the concepts of service empathy. It was Judy Rosenblum who created the improvement model that ties to market share. John Neuman helped to developed the BreakPoint prioritization scheme. James Warner and Malcom Fraser-Urquhart contributed to Demand Driven Logistics. Mark Stanton, Alan Arnett and Fred Viscovich were central to our development of the BPR implementation framework. Kate Liebfried, Rod Roy and Graham Whitney gave us practical benchmarking and Martina Platts made sense of culture change theories. Mike Blum, Grady Means, Mike Hanley and numerous other Coopers & Lybrand colleagues supported some of the case studies. Without them the book would have been the shallower, and we thank them for their help. Finally, we would like to thank Koji Inazaki and his colleagues in Tokyo for their insights into Japanese business.

We are indebted to those of our clients who had the strength of their convictions that they and their company could make a difference in the business world. We are equally thankful that they invited us along to share in their pioneering efforts. Special recognition goes to Andy Guarriello of AT&T, Werner Eisl of ABB and Larry Bossidy of AlliedSignal.

Special thanks also to Maryann Fitzgerald, Elaine Gallagher and Carol Bolger for their continued support of us during both the writing of the book and our day-to-day activities. Beth Mason of the Wilton Public Library provided valuable research. Diane Solomon is due special recognition for all of the graphics in the text as well as the coordination of all of our activities.

To Jon Zonderman fell the unenviable task of rewriting all the chapters from our rather stumbling, diverse prose and rambling discussions. Jon was the cohesive force that pulled the book together. His facile grasp of the concepts and dogged insistence upon unanimity forced us to rethink our thoughts on more than a few occasions. Special and sincere thanks from all of us.

When we set out to create this book we put down some "ways of working" together that served as guidelines for our subsequent efforts. One of the "ways" was that we were not going to write a consulting book, nor were we going to present a "How To" book. What we have attempted to do is to develop some basic tenets of how businesses are managed now and will be in the future. While we cannot claim to have performed serious academic research, we do believe that the concepts presented are born of the real world and are being further refined as we write. What follows represents our aggregate experience and observations while working with numerous leading-edge companies. We hope that the reader will enjoy the content as much as we did putting it together.

Waterford, Maine and London, England
January 1993

1
What is the New Thinking?

"I believe we have made a major mistake in our advocacy of the idea of continuous improvement. Let me explain what I mean.

"Continuous improvement is exactly the right idea if you are the world leader in everything you do. It is a terrible idea if you are lagging in the world leadership benchmark. It is probably a disastrous idea if you are far behind the world standard . . . we need rapid, quantum-leap improvement. We cannot be satisfied to lay out a plan that will move us toward the existing world standard over some protracted period of time—say 1995 or the year 2000—because if we accept such a plan, we will never be the world leader."

Paul O'Neill, Chairman ALCOA

Following the Second World War, supply strategies drove management thinking towards bureaucratic production strategies that focused on securing supply. As supply and demand came into balance, the marketing department became vital. Autocratic management was the rule around the world; many top managers were ex-military officers. Even those who were not had been acculturated to a masculine, dominant, non-participative style.

The paternalism of the past had given way to the autocratic stop-watch Taylorism writ large. Leaders like Alfred Sloan of General Motors were almost imperious—"What's good for General Motors is good for the nation," he believed.

As companies grew exponentially in the post-war years, the autocratic style became more bureaucratic, with functional heads often running their departments as fiefdoms, department heads in top management often clashing over strategy, and decisions being forced to the highest level lest the decisionmaker be cut off by someone higher up who did not agree.

But by the 1960s, a few Japanese companies were beginning to move toward process excellence in an effort to get quality enhancements and cost reductions. Leading the way in this effort was the Toyota Motor Company, with its Toyota Management System. Toyota emphasized getting the production system right, with the assumption that the market share would follow.

While this was happening, Western strategic planners stepped up their efforts to analyze, segment, and re-analyze the marketplace. In the West the market was expanding, first in the U.S. and then in Europe as it recovered from the war.

Management style was still bureaucratic, but marketing was "king." Marketing executives operated in a world of "sacred cows" and "betting the ranch." Strategy rarely, if ever, addressed manufacturing philosophies or how to achieve strategic goals through operational excellence. Planners' recommendations drove budgets, R&D, and product life cycles. Manufacturing was expected to support and follow marketing's strategic lead. Times were good and the West could afford expansion of factories and staff, just so long as the goods continued to get out the door by whatever means possible.

With the 1973 oil embargo, other Japanese companies learned process-oriented concepts from Toyota and began to convert to process-driven production. The West was still marketing hard, competing for a market that seemed to be growing ever more slowly through the 1970s. In addition, Japan was beginning to make a series of inroads into Western markets. Toyota, Nissan, and Honda all appeared in full force in the U.S. market after 1973, later in Europe. Sony and other electronics manufacturers targeted the West for their products.

In the past decade, however, Western companies have started moving toward a process orientation, using many of the techniques and philosophies the Japanese had so ably used for more than 20 years. These enablers have led to significant improvement in value-chain activities. As early as 1978, a few Western companies, feeling the impact of Japanese encroachment on their markets, began looking seriously at Japanese manufacturing techniques. By 1983 the basic principles of the Toyota Production System—what we know as Just-In-Time (JIT) manufacturing—were pretty well known in the executive suites of the West's largest companies. During the past decade, knowledge of the basic JIT principles of waste elimination, synchronous manufacturing, etc., filtered to second- and third-tier companies as well.

Companies were beginning to realize that operations are a single process, and that improving the operations process (usually manufacturing, but sometimes delivery of a service such as processing an insurance claim) can lead to competitive strength.

Today, most Western companies are still using the process orientation in a tactical sense, improving their own operations. Few have been able to extend the improvements gained through such labors beyond the business's own four walls to

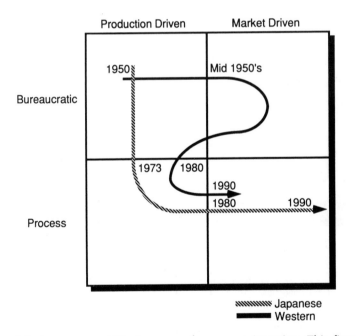

Figure 1.1 *Japanese and Western use of process orientation. This figure is based on the work of Giorgio Merli, a partner in the management consulting firm Alberto Galgano & Associati. It appears in his book* Total Manufacturing Management: Production Organization for the 1990s; *originally published in Italian in 1987, an English version was published by Productivity Press in 1990.*

make them truly strategic weapons. On the other hand, the Japanese, who have been involved in process-oriented production since the 1970s, have been leveraging their expertise in the marketplace for a decade or more. These dynamics can be seen in Figure 1.1.

Regardless of whether a company operates in a fast-moving consumer goods area such as soaps, shampoos or food; in industrial products such as bulk chemicals, steel or machine tools; or in services such as banking, insurance or consumer information, leading organizations around the world are being driven to rethink their businesses and orient toward processes. Doing this forces them to quantify the business's efforts by the four new "value metrics"—improved product *quality* and/or *service*, reduced *cycle time*, and reduced *cost* to the customer, while at the same time increasing the speed of innovation and new-product development. Figure 1.2 shows these new value metrics in greater detail.

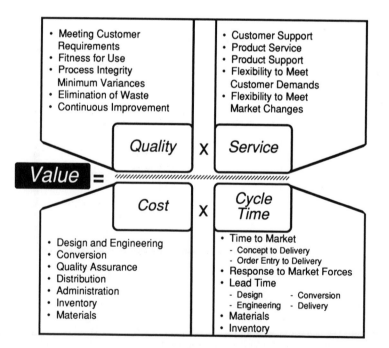

Figure 1.2 *Customer "value" criteria.*

How corporate executives perceive what is driving them to radically reengineer their businesses is the subject of Chapter 2, Why the New Thinking? They are driven by the customer; by competition; by cost; by technology shifts; even by shareholders. Politics, economics, legislation, and regulations often make the rethinking more urgent, although they do not drive it *per se*.

Once executives engage in the new thinking, they are driven toward determining how they can "defunctionalize" the organization and realign it in a process orientation. This is the subject of Chapter 3, Understanding Processes.

THE PROCESS-ORIENTATION FAMILY

The need has clearly arisen for the development and use of new ways of thinking of value-chain improvements in the operation of industrial and service enterprises, ways that focus not on improvement for the sake of improvement, but rather on improvement as the impetus for making rapid and even radical strides in the marketplace.

The question becomes one of how a business can use the power of process-oriented production concepts—what Western companies learned in the 1980s under the rubric of Just-In-Time (JIT) manufacturing and Total Quality Management (TQM)—and leverage those concepts in the marketplace.

These process-oriented concepts are far more than simply inventory management, as many still think of JIT. The three process-orientation philosophies of Just-In-Time manufacturing; Total Quality Management; and our new addition, *BreakPoint Business Process Reengineering*, are of one family.

Just-In-Time manufacturing is a unified philosophy that calls for a total reorganization of operations activities in order to minimize wasted, "non-value-adding" activities, align operations, and balance operations to demand. It utilizes the technical enablers of "pull" systems to have one operation pull work from the upstream operation rather than upstream operations pushing work (and inventory) downstream, and focuses heavily on lead time reduction. In JIT, improvements are focused on individual functions (usually beginning with manufacturing), and continuous improvement is the watchword.

Total Quality Management seeks to create an atmosphere in which "doing it right the first time" becomes the goal, where quality is designed and built into each activity rather than being inspected in after the fact. It is heavily white collar oriented, and the focus is often one that uses changes in organizational culture to drive the entire effort. The focus is on reducing the cost of quality, and it also seeks to instill a continuous improvement mindset.

Business Process Reengineering (BPR), although a close relative, seeks radical rather than merely continuous improvement. It escalates the efforts of JIT and TQM to make process orientation a strategic tool and a core competence of the organization. BPR concentrates on core business processes, and uses the specific techniques within the JIT and TQM "toolboxes" as enablers, while broadening the process vision. BPR drives corporate metrics, causing them to focus on external measures of success such as improved market share.

BPR pushes the JIT and TQM philosophies both upstream and downstream to the customer and the supplier in order to magnify their impact and take them outside the company's four walls, in order either to control the supply chain more effectively or to reach the market more effectively. In either case, the effort should yield results that improve operational effectiveness to such an extent that it provides new opportunities in the marketplace.

These approaches and their impact on business operations take on a real sense of urgency for companies as they migrate from a national to a regional (e.g. pan-European) scale and finally to a global scale.

In order to take a company used to operating in the current state and move it to process orientation, the leaders need to step back and "break the china," then put the pieces back together again in a new way. Not only must corporate leaders discover and eliminate waste, but they need to challenge the very purposes, principles, and assumptions on which their businesses are based.

Most companies today are quality conscious, with a basic understanding and commitment to TQM principles that allow operational personnel to make decisions regarding quality. Many companies are also becoming increasingly efficient, with some adherence to JIT principles of searching for and minimizing waste, questioning whether activities add value, and trying to balance operational activities to minimize bottlenecks and work-in-process inventory buildup.

Despite this, most Western companies remain *highly bureaucratic*, with departments acting individually and "throwing over the wall" to the next department designs, information, product, and most of all problems. Different functions measure work and success in different ways and, therefore, have different goals and objectives. Because of these self-perceived differences, whether conscious or not, barriers to overall business effectiveness are raised and turf is jealously guarded.

This kind of organizational linking needs to be broken apart and rebuilt as a process-oriented business, where everyone understands the ultimate goals, the ways of getting there, and the way in which success will be measured; where everyone regards working in cross-functional teams as the norm; where everyone understands and appreciates the value others add to the organization; and where everyone knows that the key goal is to produce a service or product that the marketplace perceives to be the best.

For companies to capture and maintain marketplace dominance, a new definition of operational excellence needs to be created, one that allows companies to destroy all of their preconceived paradigms about how business should be done, and begin anew; this is what we mean by *breaking the china*. This new creation must be internally driven but externally focused. Every business activity must have a connection upstream and/or downstream so that the customer or supplier, or both, receives an extraordinary degree of value from the company's relationship and so a sense of inescapability and/or symbiosis is generated.

THE OLD WAY VERSUS THE NEW WAY

While many companies have made great strides in improving their operations within their own four walls, they continue to be constrained by the old ways of thinking. But these old ways simply will not make it in the new world.

The functional approach fails to see how operational excellence cuts across almost every activity not only within a business, but across its suppliers and customers. While continuous improvement programs espouse the customer as their basis, too often they aim only at internal, functionally defined, improvements. This may be part of the reason why, in two separate 1991 surveys by national consulting firms, more than 80 percent of U.S. chief operating officers (COOs) were disappointed in the results of their companies' TQM efforts. In Coopers & Lybrand's 1991 *Made in the U.K.* survey, 14 percent of U.K. COOs were disappointed.

There are probably a few reasons for these vast differences:

- There appears to be a higher expectation of such efforts in the United States, where senior executives often become very excited about such ideas without thinking through the effort involved in making them succeed.
- Worker/management relations in the two countries differ greatly, which may lead U.K. business leaders who believe workers need to participate in improvement efforts to define even modestly better relations as "success."
- Quality improvements in Europe are often defined as writing procedures for companies to measure up to ISO 9000 standards, which many U.S. business leaders see as a false measure of quality.

Whatever the true reason, the point is that there is often dissatisfaction with traditional TQM efforts, and we believe the fact that they fail to break down functional barriers and truly engage individuals in improving processes that touch the supplier and the customer is at the heart of this dissatisfaction, whether or not it is articulated that way.

Traditional accounting and performance measures are inappropriate in the new world. Profitability and cash flows are not the only business drivers that need to be extended to cover such areas as market standing, speed of response, flexibility, and meeting or exceeding customer expectations. And assets are far more than working capital; they include people, corporate culture, technologies, brands, tricks of the trade, etc.

Information systems on top of functional thinking and traditional accounting and performance measures often move the wrong information faster, and fail to provide employees with the depth and structure of information required for them to be truly effective in all aspects of their work. Mainframe computers drive management toward increased bureaucracy, they systematize and invest in the old ways of thinking, which then become ingrained in "new" technology.

Figure 1.3 shows how the "price of admission" in this new world has changed. While in 1970 companies could effectively compete on the basis of product characteristics, today time-to-market, speed and service are being added to the armament that includes quality, innovation, functionality and cost on the list of "must do's" to remain competitive.

While many companies are working hard to bring their organizations up to necessary levels of competence in the areas of time-to-market, speed and service, leading-edge companies are pushing on to the next generation of the basis of competition—market differentiation in terms of flexibility and what we call "virtuality."

Virtuality defines the ability to create a partnership across companies throughout the entire supply chain—companies band together synergistically so that they can dominate the market. Process management taken to its highest level, therefore, cuts not only across departments and functions in one company, or even across separate plants owned by the same company that perform different parts of the core business

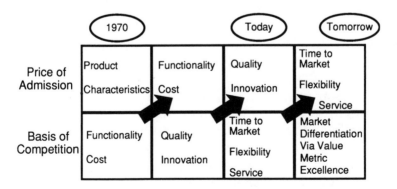

Figure 1.3 *The basis of competition is changing.*

process, but literally across all the different companies that make up the supply chain.

An example of this is Wal-Mart, described in more detail in Chapter 2, where the company has created an elaborate system of partnership with its suppliers. Another is a manufacturer of material for carpeting, described in Chapter 5, which has created a partnership with the company that turns its fibers into rugs in an attempt to deliver custom-ordered carpet to a retailer in one week from the order.

A QUICK RECAP: JAPAN LEADS THE WAY

It seems that for 20 years the Japanese have been driving the rapidly increasing price of admission. Since Japan began rebuilding its economy after the Second World War, industrial leadership focused on competing with and beating Western, especially U.S., companies. With that very simple strategy, they set about finding and utilizing the tactical tools that would enable them to do that.

The leader in this regard was Toyota, which spent 20 years or more designing the Toyota Production System, which packaged the principles of what we now call JIT. After the first oil embargo of 1973, companies throughout Japan began to emulate Toyota's lean production, fanaticism with eliminating waste in manufacturing processes, and constant drive to increase quality.

European and U.S. companies, somewhat less affected by the tripling of energy prices, were slower to catch on; many were shocked into reality in the late 1970s and early 1980s as Japanese companies began to capture significant market share—especially in North America—in cars and consumer electronics.

U.S. companies especially continued through the 1960s and 1970s to focus on refining strategy, focusing on marketing and the portfolio theory of business—putting more energy into determining where to compete rather than how. Slowly, beginning in the early 1980s, they began to refocus their energies on creating better capabilities within manufacturing operations, creating better engineering organizations, rationalizing suppliers, improving response time and "service empathy," and generally tightening operating standards.[*]

But it was already too late. Since the mid-1970s, Japanese companies had routinely been cutting into the market share of Western, especially American, companies. The tactical tools had turned into strategic weapons.

The response of many business and government leaders was to blame low wages, Japanese culture, patent theft and a host of other real or imagined Japanese practices. But a few in Western business saw that the Japanese—regardless of the other issues—were catching on to the tactical process-oriented tools of JIT and TQM that were changing the basis of competition. By the early 1980s Western companies such as Hewlett-Packard, IBM and Airbus began to implement what Richard Schoenberg called in a book of the same name "Japanese Manufacturing Techniques" and to beat the Japanese in head-to-head competition.

WHY JIT AND TQM ALONE DO NOT DELIVER THE GOODS

Because they have become part of the price of admission, the mere adoption of tactical process-oriented principles—and even their successful implementation—does not bring companies to the cutting edge of international competition. While over time these various tools and techniques create vast improvements in internal effectiveness, they cannot provide the means to break out from the deadlocked market competitive position—once everybody is playing the same game, a position of essential parity is reached.

Figure 1.4 shows the position map of a company before implementing tactical process orientation. The current company has a share of market that can be measured, and has a

---

[*] The term "service empathy" was first used by William Band, a partner with the Coopers & Lybrand Consulting Group in Toronto, Canada. He leads the firm's Centre for Excellence in Customer Satisfaction and is the author of *Creating Value for Customers: Designing and Implementing a Total Corporate Strategy*, published by John Wiley & Sons, New York, in 1991; ISBN 0-471-52593-6.

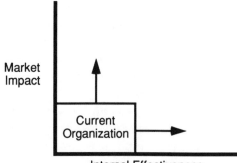

Figure 1.4 *Internal effectiveness/market impact before implementing tactical process orientation.*

level of internal effectiveness. (It produces at a given cost with a given level of quality, and does so in a fashion that can be quantified by the marketplace in comparison to competitors.)

Figure 1.5 shows what happens after implementation of tactical process techniques and principles. Internal effectiveness is usually substantially improved. Work flows more smoothly, often producing a production flow that more closely resembles constant demand, thus reducing finished-goods inventory and the related costs. By more closely linking operations, work-in-process inventory and its costs are reduced. The rapidity of work flowing from one point to another rather than sitting in

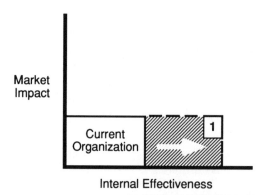

Figure 1.5 *Internal effectiveness/market impact after implementation of tactical process techniques: Level 1.*

long queues, and smaller production runs, also allow for more immediate feedback about quality and the ability of employees at any step in the operation immediately to envision a "better way" to do something.

Yet even with these immediate and often far-reaching improvements in internal effectiveness that can be achieved using these tools and techniques, there is usually little or no improvement in market share. Although there is often significant short- and medium-term improvement in the company's bottom line, eventually executives realize that the key to long-term company health is not continually squeezing out cost but rather growing the market share or finding new markets.

This is the plan designed by Larry Bossidy, Chairman and CEO of AlliedSignal. First he streamlined the business by cutting out layers of management. Then he divested the company of divisions that were not performing at the top of their market. Finally, he has mandated a corporate-wide Business Process Reengineering effort that emphasizes speed, with the aim of helping the company achieve its goal of 8 percent real growth per year.

An achievement of this magnitude will be remarkable for AlliedSignal, which gains 80 percent of its revenues from the automotive and aerospace sectors, both of which are expected to remain depressed through much of the 1990s.

Most companies are left after all of their internal-effectiveness improvements with the strategic issue posed in Figure 1.6; that question, simply put, is: "What do I do with the 40–50 percent excess capacity that history shows is always discovered through the effective implementation of tactical process-oriented techniques?"

The response to the strategic issue can be market driven by manipulating the price/volume curves within the existing marketplace, or value-chain driven by closing or mothballing facilities, marketing the capacity of the core technology, or back sourcing—bringing back in-house the manufacture of components or subassemblies previously subcontracted out.

When all is said and done, the result of all of this effort is essentially marketplace parity and, as more and more companies are coming to realize, *parity is not winning*— achieving parity guarantees that a company will have to continue

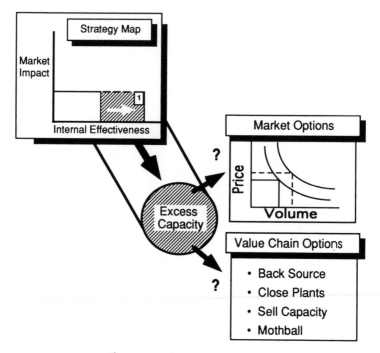

Figure 1.6   *First strategic issue.*

running as hard as it can just to keep up. Increasingly, companies are determining that the only way to compete successfully is to capture and maintain dominance in the marketplace, to *create the rules that others have to play by*. Regis McKenna, the public relations guru who to a great degree developed Apple Computer's marketing strategy, observed that *market leadership is ownership*.

THE NEED TO MASTER THE ELEMENTS

Unfortunate though it might seem, it is impossible for companies to implement successfully BreakPoint Business Process Reengineering without having first undertaken one of the tactical process-oriented techniques. Companies must spend some time thinking about processes and how to improve them before they can be radical and work toward reengineering core business processes.

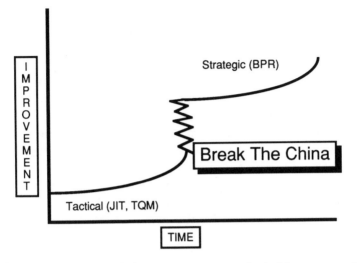

Figure 1.7   A company's journey to process-oriented improvement.

The lessons learned from these earlier efforts in the areas of rigorous analysis of operations to eliminate waste and non-value-adding steps, teambuilding and cross-functional teamwork, employee empowerment, doing it right the first time, and a host of other activities, are invaluable. The dedication one develops through these efforts to questioning how things are done, and why they are done, is also a necessary prerequisite for the more intense and rigorous process of "breaking the china" needed for successful BreakPoint BPR.

Figure 1.7 shows the journey a company might make toward process-oriented improvement, working on a tactical level, then stopping and "breaking the china" before progressing to the strategic level of operational excellence.

BUSINESS PROCESS REENGINEERING, WITH OR WITHOUT BREAKPOINTS

Business Process Reengineering is, by definition, the means by which an organization can achieve radical change in performance as measured by cost, cycle time, service, and quality, by the application of a variety of tools and techniques that focus on the business as a set of related customer-oriented core business processes rather than a set of organizational functions.

A core business process, as distinct from other processes, is a set of linked activities that both crosses functional boundaries and, when carried out in concert, addresses the needs and expectations of the marketplace and drives the organization's capabilities. Reengineering of these core business processes takes place when operational, technical, and business knowledge are used in a unified way in order to achieve sustainable competitive advantage.

A BreakPoint is the achievement of excellence in one or more of the "value metrics"—the values the market puts on products and services—to the extent that the marketplace clearly recognizes the advantage and where the ensuing result is a disproportionate and sustained increase in market share.

Some people confuse a core business process with a core technology. For instance, if you ask an electronics company executive to describe a core process, he will likely say "board stuffing." This is, in fact, a core technology—every electronics company must stuff boards, or get a subcontractor to stuff boards, in order to build product. But board stuffing is not a core process in the way that, say, maintenance of the supply chain is for the automotive industry. There is really no ability for an electronics manufacturer to differentiate or create market advantage based on its ability to stuff boards. Board stuffing is, in fact, a price of admission.

But reengineering the supply chain process in, for example, the automotive industry could lead to staggering changes in market dynamics, and is thus a core process. The manufacturer of catalytic converters discovered an opportunity to reduce the cost of goods by 41 percent and reduce a 250 day inventory float that existed because an OEM mismanaged the supply chain.

One way to think about the differentiation between core business processes and core technologies is that a core business process combines both physical activity—the heart of core technology—with information flow, and addresses the needs and desires of the marketplace.

A limited number of core business processes—usually no more than half a dozen or so—can be identified in any company or industry, and enhancing any of those processes can lead to business improvement. The evaluation of these processes to determine the best candidates for reengineering and the methodology for reengineering a core business process will be taken up in Chapter 4, Putting the China Back Together. Defining which processes are core business processes and which are not is the subject of Chapter 3, Understanding Processes.

Through this rigorous evaluation of these core business processes and their ability to increase the perceived value in the marketplace, a process may be identified which, when exploited to its fullest, creates a BreakPoint. A BreakPoint occurs when the market share moves disproportionately upward as a result of a perceived improvement in a universally understood value set. The end result is that this new Break-Point business process then sets the market profile and/or service requirements for the industry.

Figure 1.8 shows how the innovative nature of a BreakPoint leads not only to ultra-enhanced internal effectiveness, but to a market impact. By developing a vision of true value-chain excellence that is beyond industry best practice, the internal organization is stretched to create an action plan of step-by-step improvements that in and of themselves can be potential BreakPoints.

For instance, if the market read—the analysis of what the market finds important when deciding among competitors—

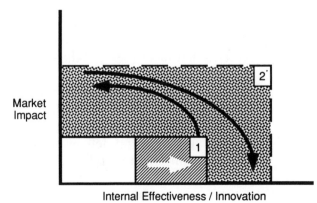

Figure 1.8 Level 2—BreakPoint.

indicates that lead time is a potential BreakPoint, then significant lead time reduction requires that all non-value-adding activities are eliminated, that quality defects approach a level of *Six Sigma*—three parts per million (3 ppm)—and that the customer becomes integral to the value-chain process. The result will be tremendous cost reduction, unbeatable quality, and a service alliance with the customer that is impervious to competitive thrusts.

In the case of Graniterock, a California "manufacturer" of rocks for roads and highways* and a winner of the 1992 Malcolm Baldrige Award, this means producing rock products with such high quality and uniformity that they exceed standards set by the California Department of Transportation, The Federal Aviation Administration, the Federal Highway Administration, and a host of other state and national regulatory agencies. The company offers training and opportunity for advancement to all 400 of its employees, 250 of whom are unionized.

The company is in an industry where products are essentially undifferentiated—commodity; where much of the work is public sector and done through bid; and where cost has historically been thought of as the only competitive factor. But the company has successfully differentiated itself in the construction industry through its quality efforts; its crushed-rock products are thought of as superior.

The company has defined the following as its nine corporate objectives:

1 *Customer satisfaction and service.* To earn the respect of our customers by providing them in a timely manner with the products and services that meet their needs and solve their problems.
2 *Safety.* To operate all granite rock facilities with safety as the primary goal. Meeting schedules or production volume is secondary.
3 *Production efficiency.* To produce and deliver our products at the lowest possible cost consistent with the other objectives.

---

*The Graniterock Company has worked extensively with the author, consultant and presenter Nancy K. Austin, to whom we are grateful for permission to reproduce this material.

4 *Financial performance and growth*. Our growth is limited only by our profits and the ability of Graniterock people to develop creatively and implement business growth strategies.
5 *Community commitment*. To be good citizens in each of the communities in which we operate.
6 *Management*. To foster initiative, creativity, and commitment by allowing the individual greater freedom of action (in deciding how to do a job) in attaining defined objectives (the goals set by management).
7 *Profit*. To provide a profit to fund growth and to provide resources needed to fund achievement of our other objectives.
8 *Product quality assurance*. To provide products which provide lasting value to our customers, and conform to state, federal, or local government specifications.
9 *People*. To provide an environment in which each person in the organization gains a sense of satisfaction and accomplishment from personal achievements, to recognize individual and team accomplishments, and to reward individuals based upon their contributions and job performance.

Graniterock uses "management by fact" to constantly measure performance versus the company's baseline goals and benchmarks, which coincide with the nine corporate objectives.

The culture of the company's efforts is so ingrained that, when asked by an outsider what makes the company's crushed-rock product different from the rock of any other company, one truck driver said, "it's the molecules."

THE FINAL STEP ALONG THE VALUE CHAIN

Once a company is well along the path of implementing improvements in the value-chain elements, it is possible to take advantage of these improvements either to enhance its position in related markets or even to enter new markets, as shown in Figure 1.9.

An example is a manufacturer of tobacco packaging, formerly captive to its parent company. The company's process involves rolling aluminum foil to a four-thousandths of an inch thickness,

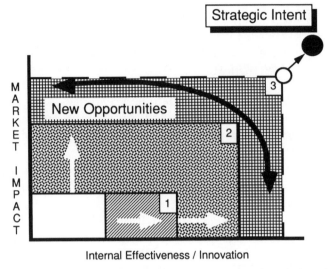

Figure 1.9 Opportunities arising from improved value-chain elements: Level 3.

laminating printed paper to the aluminum, then sandwiching it between polypropylene layers. The process is performed on a multistation machine that used to require up to 36 hours to change over from one product run to another.

By analyzing the setup process with classic JIT techniques, the company determined that the *daringly pragmatic* vision of what could be was a changeover time of one hour or less. Recognizing that every time there was a changeover there would be a potential of 35 hours of capacity or significantly smaller lot sizes, a strategy developed to take some of the increased performance each way.

Smaller lot sizes allowed the process to capture much traditional JIT improvement—vast reductions in the amount of finished-goods inventory through smaller lot sizes that more closely matched the numbers of cigarettes produced under each brand name—while at the same time finding a place in new yet related markets in florist foil, airline peanut packaging, etc. The company could now deliver small lot sizes at competitive price; in the past, because of the long changeover times, customers would have had to accept weeks of supply that would cost them space to store, potential spoilage from damage, and may have caused cash-flow problems.

By reading the market before the major changeover break-through was achieved, the company was able to achieve market segmented BreakPoint, as well as producing huge savings in its core process. The company went from 90 percent captive to 60 percent external, and has improved its parent company's bottom line through reducing inventory expenses and increasing revenues.

Another example is Omark, the maker of chain saw blades. An early advocate of JIT in the early 1980s, Omark had 85 percent of the market at the beginning of its operational improvement efforts. It maintained dominance by rigorously streamlining its operations via the application of JIT and, more recently, Business Process Reengineering throughout the supply chain. In the mid-1980s, the company began developing new products only partially related to the chain saw business in order to market excess capacity in its core technology.

Both of these examples show how companies take creative approaches to the excess capacity that is almost always a result of these aggressive process management efforts.

A full discussion of how to determine potential BreakPoints and then test for which ones to try to effect in the near or long term appears in Chapter 5, Searching for BreakPoints.

Clearly, it is in many businesses' interest to reengineer core business processes to achieve internal effectiveness above and beyond what has been attained through JIT and TQM. But not all companies will actually take Business Process Reengineering to the level of the rigorous search for potential BreakPoints and then make the efforts it takes to capitalize on one or more of those Breakpoints.

There are three major reasons for this:

1   Operational excellence will never be viewed in and of itself by the market as a BreakPoint. For example, the fast food business requires quality food served rapidly at a fair price. However, the process of preparing and serving the food is, on rigorous analysis, not a differentiator. Rather, the process of acquisition or de-acquisition of land, and the management and utilization of that land can significantly increase the fast food company's profits. In short, fast food providers are really in the real estate business, and as in any

aspect of real estate, the three key success factors are location, location, and location.

2   Some companies do not see the need to go for BreakPoints if they can maintain what are considered reasonable margins and profits, even if only in the short run. For example, most U.S. automakers have been complacent even in the context of declining markets. Ford, however, has been working supply chain issues (not necessarily under the formal rubric of Business Process Reengineering, although some explicit reengineering work has taken place) for years—most notably with the advent of the Taurus/Sable line. The results have born out the concept; via BPR Ford gained over four market points during the late 1980s.

   Two processes stand out. The design of the Taurus/Sable depended heavily on Quality Function Deployment (QFD) techniques. And via a partnering with key suppliers in the spare parts chain (virtuality), Ford improved servicing of spare parts from a 93 percent fill rate to better than 98 percent, significantly reducing lead time and closing a number of distribution centers.

3   The key reason most companies do not look for BreakPoints is that they are, simply, timid, lacking the competitive fire that turns a routine reengineering effort into a vision of what the company could be and a quest to get there. Others fear the significant risk of disruption to the day-to-day activities of the business that searching for BreakPoints could have if the effort were not managed properly.

Most companies do not come to Business Process Reengineering with the idea of BreakPoints in mind. Most, in fact, seek help for yet another cost-cutting effort, and most focus on non-core processes such as the monthly financial closings as the place to cut costs.

For instance, at one pharmaceutical company, it took an entire month to close the books on the previous month's activities. Many companies find themselves in this dilemma, spending effort on anticipating this month's closing rather than performing last month's, so there are better projections but a more drawn-out process of getting actual figures. The pharmaceutical company did a good job reducing the time to perform the closing, but it would have been better off reducing the research and Food and Drug Administration approval or Good Manufacturing Practices validation processes, which are core to the business they are in, rather than the routine supporting process of performing financial closings.

It takes a while, but many companies are learning that costs can be cut in core processes if those processes are reengineered to focus on the new value metrics of quality, time, cost, and service.

A notable exception, a company that came to the concept of business process reengineering with the specific purpose of seeking out a BreakPoint, was the Motorola pager business. The company can now turn around a uniquely configured pager—from order entry through manufacture to shipping—in a few hours. In Motorola's case, it was forced to think radically because it simply could not compete on price with Japanese pagers; but the company had in place people who were willing and able to think radically. These qualities will be explored in Chapter 8 on organizing and managing the BPR effort and transition to a process-oriented company.

SEEKING BREAKPOINTS "BY ACCIDENT"

Many companies are driven to reengineer core business processes when faced with the realization of what the marketplace demands. In the process of reengineering core business processes, the company finds that while working to deliver the "must do's" to the demanding marketplace, excitement within the organization at the improvements being made causes people—especially corporate leadership—to begin thinking about the "can do's" the company could deliver to the market, and the search for BreakPoint begins, as seen in Figure 1.10.

"Must do's" are the things companies must do well just to be a player in an industry, the current basis of competition that the industry, competitors and customers force on a business. "Can do's" are the things a particular business can accomplish given its particular organization and processes. Chapter 5, Searching for BreakPoints, will go into detail on how to determine from your processes what your company is capable of.

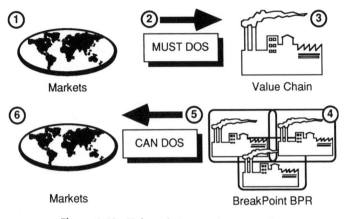

Figure 1.10 *Value chain–market interplay.*

The intensity with which marketing efforts for years have segmented and resegmented markets has put increasing pressures on operational activities. A prime example is the proliferation of airline rate structures, or the different test procedures necessary for each customer's integrated circuit requirements. While customers are important and must be listened to, marketing operations often allow market desires that are really not all that strong to drive their companies' operations, rather than looking to operations to create a new or enhanced value to the marketplace in terms of one of the value metrics defined.

Take the Baskins Robbins ice cream concept, for example. At any time, the company produces 31 flavors of ice cream. This means that the factory only has 31 products to make at any one time. The flavors change throughout the year due to: (i) change in season; (ii) creativity of the research department; and (iii) response to marketplace favorites.

The company competes on the continued high quality of the ice cream itself, as well as the extremely high quality of those 31 flavors and their originality.

Ken Olson, the founder and long-time CEO of Digital Equipment Company, often said, "We say the customer is always right. But the customer is not always right." For many years Olson's company was able to deliver not merely what the customer wanted, but what the customer would value in the future.

The tobacco packaging company could have looked to the market's apparent love for low price and decided to compete on that basis, but instead it chose to go after market share by offering smaller lot sizes, and thus used the value metric of flexibility to meet customer demand.

Business Process Reengineering forces corporate leaders to take a radical approach to the way their business is positioned, organized, and run. Only those leaders have the stature to overturn deliberately the paradigms their businesses have come to accept as the norms; to throw out sacred cows and look for new ways to define the conduct of their affairs.

Once this is done, it becomes easier to envision how one can move one's company from the "must do's" to the "can do's."

One integrated circuit (IC) manufacturer, while studying its strategy, undertook to identify what the value chain "must do" to remain competitive five years hence. The report named five basic "must do's" in order to be a player in the future:

- delivery reliability +/− one day;
- two-week lead time;
- on-line order status inquiry;
- negotiable special terms and prices;
- flexibility for volume changes.

Examination of the last three elements shows that customers were unable to manage their own manufacturing activities and were, therefore, trying to push the responsibility for excellence upstream to the supplier. Furthermore, the market read indicates that the customer did not know what an IC manufacturer was capable of doing.

Detailed examination of the IC value chain reveals that order entry, assembly and test, and delivery to the customer can be accomplished in four days if the supplier sells capacity that is synchronized with the customer's actual daily total usage, regardless of item mix. By locking in key customers there is little need for the level of flexibility for volume changes and status reporting abilities identified. The avoidance of additional internal costs incurred by the customer should negate the perceived need for negotiating special terms.

By offering four-day delivery, the IC manufacturer can distance himself from the competition. By working hard and reengineering core processes in order to drive the value chain to its ultimate capability, the IC manufacturer is able to reap a disproportionate gain in market share. Equally as important, assuming that all competitors can obtain the same information and have relatively the same understanding of the market, the competition will put significant resources into developing a two-week throughput time. That process will be very different from the four-day process and it will be extremely difficult, if not impossible, to collapse into a four-day process without another reengineering effort.

By analyzing what the value chain ultimately can be and not merely what it needs to be to achieve competitive parity, potential BreakPoints appear. The potential BreakPoints can then be further analyzed to see which are easier to accomplish and what the relative increase in market reaction will be to each. A value-chain BreakPoint strategy is based upon clearly defined and linked visions of the market and the internal effectiveness of the company. The vision is "daringly pragmatic" and has the customer as the driver.

LIFE IN THE NEW WAY: KEY ENABLERS OF BPR

In the world of process management and defunctionalization, management has to have a whole new outlook on the pieces that make up a company: the people, management and leadership skills, organizational culture, the need for expertise, the need for faster decisionmaking and instantaneous reaction to marketplace stimuli, asset management, and performance measurements. The old bureaucratic way of thinking of these issues simply will not make it in the new way.

People

It is axiomatic that people are a business's greatest asset. But too often this notion is merely empty rhetoric. Companies that seek to create new paradigms, to defunctionalize and seek totally process-driven work, and to seek and effect BreakPoints, need to make sure they take full advantage of their greatest resource.

The human capital development within BreakPoint-oriented companies must go beyond producing merely "empowered" employees to the development of truly "Renaissance" employees who can move from one business process development team to another, who can take their special skills and learning and enhance a team working on any project, and who can in turn increase skills and learning in each process-development assignment they undertake and take it with them to the next task.

Management and Leadership

In a similar way, the corporate or strategic business unit leadership must be "re-suited." Leaders will no longer manage through functional executives, but rather through the directors of identified core business processes. Leaders must manage the *angst* of radicalization while allowing core business process directors to lead the operational charge.

Implicit in this is that leaders in companies that work in the new way must be technically knowledgeable in order to understand the implications of process-oriented operations. When one looks at examples of companies at the forefront of Business Process Reengineering, one often sees leaders who rose through the technical ranks rather than finance or marketing. And those leaders with finance or marketing backgrounds have been exposed to the tactical tools and techniques of operational excellence and have grasped their power.

Organizational Culture

The combination of people and leadership/management style is the essence of organizational culture. The kind of organization that is most likely to be successful at Business Process Reengineering is one that already has a high degree of:

- leadership that can create a vision, articulate values, and create a climate in which business unit executives, managers

and line personnel can all grow, flourish, and have an
impact on the way work is done;
- shared values;
- teamwork at all levels;
- constituency relationships, especially with shareholders,
customers, and suppliers;
- change and the desire to dominate the market.

Working to set up the organizational preconditions for
successful Business Process Reengineering is discussed in
Chapter 8, Organizing and Managing for Success.

Functional Expertise

Business Process Reengineering seeks as its ultimate goal the
most complete defunctionalization of the business possible
consistent with corporate strategy. Clearly, this cannot happen
overnight, so the aim of Business Process Reengineering is to
continue breaking down the functional biases under which
most managers and executives operate, and to drive more and
more of the business's operations into a process orientation.

But even in the radically defunctionalized company, there
will always be the need for expertise and knowledge of people
from the former functions; the ultimate goal is for companies
to be core-business-process driven with small cadres of
functional experts who advise many business-process teams
in intricacies of what used to be functions, and who undertake
the required functional work such as health and safety, tax
compliance, financial reporting, etc.

Stockpiling

Stockpiling, which will be discussed in Chapter 5, Searching
for BreakPoints, is when a company finds two BreakPoints it
can achieve, takes one now and puts the process capability for
the other "on the shelf" to bring to bear when the marketplace
reacts and catches up with the first BreakPoint.

It is interesting to note the difference between some Japanese automotive manufacturers and their U.S. counterparts. The Japanese develop technological breakthroughs independent of the immediate application. For instance, if they develop a new carburation system they will debug the new technology and put it on the shelf, or incorporate it into existing or new models at a later date when the market requires the next technological step (technology stockpiling).

Western designers will incorporate the new technology, along with many others, into a new model immediately. The process debugging occurs on the fly. Not only do the Japanese have the advantage of managing the rollout of new technology, but they significantly reduce the design-to-market cycle.

Instantaneous Reaction

The ultimate principle of this delayered, team-oriented, process-driven organization is that simpler is better, that the more direct the contact between the marketplace and business operations the more immediate the reaction to marketplace stimuli can be. This organization will be able to read the constantly changing market stimuli and react almost instantaneously, reaching to the shelf for one of its stockpiled BreakPoints when available and reengineering processes to discover new BreakPoints when necessary.

The New Assets and Their Management

This organization must take a new view of asset management. As BPR efforts progress, one of the first phenomena is excess capacity. As processes are reengineered, even more capacity is discovered.

The most frequent response is downsizing. While this may be appropriate, the remaining assets must be viewed differently. Multifacility operations may want to downsize all locations instead of closing one, in order to maintain flexibility.

In addition, capital equipment justifications cannot be made on a stand-alone basis. Rather, the decisions are based on the necessity to achieve the strategic results coming from the reengineered process objectives. In the new way of operating, more equipment will be simple, dedicated, and disposable.

But what really happens is that a new definition of assets occurs, no longer focusing on financial and physical assets. In the new way of operating, people, brands, intellectual property, value-metric excellence, and process technology are all assets. The business unit executive, the field general on the ground who drives the BPR effort, must take responsibility for developing, enhancing, renewing, and regenerating those assets.

Performance Indicators

Since reengineered processes are trans-functional, most key performance indicators are inappropriate. The new way of operating requires only four business performance indicators:

- quality;
- lead time;
- cost;
- service.

One consumer products company has 520 operational indicators—many conflicting with each other—that the corporation watches every quarter. For example, distribution is measured on "effective use of cubage," i.e. are the shelves full? Since distribution drives the production schedule, the factory is constantly making product that is not required and that in turn forces discounted sales to retailers in order to comply with another metric, minimal inventory, to say nothing of margin.

Another company went into an improvement effort with one metric that looked at how many people were trained in the improvement tools and techniques. After two years, the company had responded to the metric—all 2500 employees had been trained—but there were no actual improvements implemented.

The purpose in reducing the metrics to four simple ones is that everyone in an organization can focus on them at all times; they can be easily displayed and understood; and, most importantly, they drive the desired results asked for by the aggregate 520 measures, without running the risk of conflicting metrics, metrics that do not really produce significant analysis but rather produce a lot of noise, and a host of other problems that can arise when activities are over-measured.

BPR AND GLOBALIZATION

Current frameworks for operating businesses globally often do not take advantage of the basic operational excellence within a company. Too often, companies working in the global context have decentralized their operations, often assigning profit-and-loss responsibility on a country or regional basis (the equivalent of functional orientation) and relegating breakthroughs to the local level. (Of course, because of differences in regulations and taxation, even process-oriented companies may need to work in a local-company structure.)

In the new way of thinking, where businesses are organized in a process-oriented fashion, profit-and-loss responsibility will fall to business-process units that key on operations, and assets and capacity will be managed more actively on a worldwide basis, with resources of different types balanced in time and across borders.

Basically, the larger the company is, and the more its operations cross borders, the higher the imperative for it to undertake Business Process Reengineering. This will be described in more detail in Chapter 7, Process Management in Large Businesses.

2
Why the New Thinking?

Breaking the china is not a new concept, only a new way of describing an old phenomenon. Throughout history, in business as well as in politics and other areas, world leaders have always broken the mold; those who win are generally those who take the radical view. The Toyota Production System that sought, through a host of new concepts, to eliminate waste in the production process, and Ford's introduction of the moving assembly line and standardized parts to replace custom-built cars 40 years earlier, are clear examples of the search for new ways of operating.

Similarly, Sam Walton's creation of Wal-Mart Inc. and the consequent remaking of retailing in the United States is another dramatic example of how a company can change the rules of the game in an industry.

The Wal-Mart lesson is one of dynamism and aggressive emphasis on organizational practices and excellence in core business processes, one that is of great relevance to most companies today. Such luminous examples as Wal-Mart, Toyota, and Ford might imply that it is difficult, if not impossible, for other organizations to succeed in such efforts. Yet the evidence abounds that the same route is open to large numbers of organizations that think carefully and deeply about the nature of the business they are in and how they can break the competitive deadlock to change the game in their favor.

The key lies in the visionary thinking of the chief executive, who must act as a catalyst in seeking to redefine his business's operating capabilities. The precipitating factor in causing that chief executive to become a visionary can be changes in the market, legislative or regulatory changes, industry realignment, or a host of other factors. In the end, it is usually about shareholder value; if it becomes clear that shareholder value can no longer be maintained or enhanced in the existing environment, something must be done.

Of course, for such leaders as Sam Walton, who owned Wal-Mart privately and had no public shareholders, regulators or stock analysts looking over his shoulder, return on assets may be of less immediate concern. For them—and for many who must respond to stock values—there is also the drive to succeed, to do better, to drive oneself and one's organization to outstanding levels of performance.

The visionary leader also feels a level of dissatisfaction, not only with current performance but with the narrow view of traditional business strategy setting. More and more, business leaders have come up through the ranks of operational areas rather than strictly through marketing or finance, as was the case. Many of these operations-nurtured leaders have seen the success of the tactical process-oriented philosophies of JIT and TQM, and have looked for a way to bring the process philosophy into the broader realm of corporate strategy.

They, especially, have become increasingly frustrated with the old notion of strategy in which they ask the following questions:

- What do we sell?
- To whom do we sell it?
- Where do we sell it?

These corporate leaders who cut their teeth in operations want to know also:

- How do we organize and operate in order to produce it?

When William Edgerly became president of State Street Bank in Boston it was a far cry from his former life in manufacturing. But he quickly realized that moving paper through banking processes is no different than moving goods down an assembly line. Thinking of the process from the customer through the back-office activities, and then focusing on providing effective transaction processing services to other financial-service providers such as stock brokers and mutual funds, Edgerly has made State Street Bank number one in return on assets for all U.S. banks.

As more corporate leaders have come out of operations, and as more leaders not trained in operations have become familiar with the tactical process-orientation philosophies, even introducing them into corporate activities and service industries, leaders are increasingly asking that the question of *how* goods and services are provided be answered in any discussion of strategy.

In short, they are asking for in-house strategists and strategy advisors to broaden the definition of business strategy and help them think in terms of processes.

Such a drive forward to reach new heights through process orientation was evident in both Toyota and Honda as they in different ways sought to reach prominent international market positions.

At Toyota, its well-proved success in revolutionizing the production processes and delivery capabilities during the mid-1950s drove management towards increasingly lofty visions of the future, ultimately to be bigger than General Motors. At the beginning of the 1980s, Toyota set itself the interim goal of achieving 10 percent of global market share in automobiles. This was always going to be a difficult proposition. However, in an interview in mid-1991, while Soichiro Toyoda, Toyota's president, said he was not giving undue attention to that vision, data shown in Figure 2.1 shows how Toyota's ambitions had been realized.

Honda's rise as a force in the global motor industry owes much to the vision of its founder, Soichiro Honda, and his partner, Takeo Fujisawa. Initially after the Second World War the company developed superior manufacturing processes that doubled the horsepower obtainable from a four-stroke engine. While Fujisawa wanted to exploit innovative technology for commercial reasons, Honda wanted to use the higher horsepower engine to pursue one of his central ambitions in life, success in motorcycle racing. So, in 1954, Honda attended the famous Isle of Man TT races while on a visit to European car manufacturers.

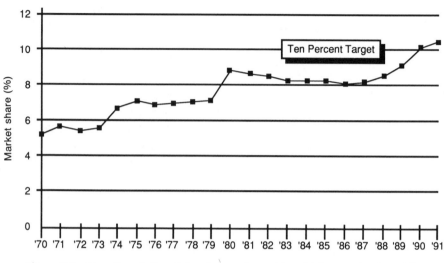

Figure 2.1 *Growth of Toyota's share of world vehicle production.* The Automotive Industry, Toyota and Japan, *1992 edition.*

Following Honda's decision to enter the race, the Japanese team was the subject of much light-hearted banter, but in 1959 the team placed sixth in the 125 cc category, and by 1961 the Japanese won both the 125 and 250 cc events.

Meanwhile, the company had commercialized its motor-cycles, becoming Japan's largest domestic manufacturer by 1955, and developing a customer base in the United Kingdom, then on the Continent and in the United States, partly as a result of publicity over the team's increasing racing successes in the late 1950s and into the 1960s.

But the technical superiority could not be capitalized on fully without Honda's focus on the core business process of creating a distribution network, understanding what customers want and creating ways to get the product to them.

In the 1960s Honda turned its expertise in engine design to other types of engines, for autos, boats and even lawn mowers. The core business process of engine design has always driven Honda's corporate strategy. Only after perfecting an engine type did the company begin manufacturing its own products—first cars and then lawnmowers. And it has refined and improved its distribution processes continually.

DRIVEN TO A VISION

Let us take a more detailed look at some of the events or changes that may drive corporate leaders to visionary thinking.

The Customer as Driver

Since all businesses have customers, it is scarcely surprising that a frequent cause for radical redefinition of business processes comes from reassessing the relationship with the customer.

In today's competitive world, the customer is no longer king; rather, he or she becomes an integral part of the team that helps define a company's core business processes, its strategies, and its competencies. Because customer needs evolve and are subject to the vagaries of convention and fashion, companies need to develop mechanisms to track customer requirements and monitor the "voice of the customer." The customer must be brought into the process as part of an alliance.

Yet, at the same time, it is necessary to monitor the "voice of the process," and quickly correct mismatches between the two, determining if customer expectations can be achieved by the process; if the process can be redesigned to achieve customer expectations; or even if the process can deliver more than the customer even knows to ask for, in which case a Breakpoint can be created.

Japanese auto, electronics and motorcycle manufacturers are renowned for having raised measurement of customer requirements to new levels. Equally, U.K. retailers such as Sainsbury's and Tesco have been able to maintain steady growth through changing economic conditions by continuously seeking to increase quality and variety of staple items such as food and drink at prices satisfactory to both customers and shareholders. They, like Wal-Mart, have rigorously sought to control the supply chain.

Sam Walton put himself in the shoes of the customer. He understood their desires—the merchandise they want when they want it and where they want it; and courteous service.

The service aspect was tackled by having stock options available to everyone; the theory being that if clerks own stock it is "their" business, as if each individual owned his or her own store.

Walton also worked hard at creating store accessibility, scouting for locations for new stores in an airplane and locating them on the outskirts of smaller cities, often between three or four medium sized communities.

To satisfy the customers' merchandise-specific desires, Walton relentlessly focused on making the inventory replenishment process the core of his competitive strategy. He defined supply-chain management as a core business process. By giving his key suppliers electronic point of sale (EPOS) information so they could track how much of every item they needed to manufacture for Wal-Mart, and when a new order of material needed to be delivered, Wal-Mart was able to eliminate the need to hold stock in its own warehouses or distribution centers and manufacturers were able to run their own operations more efficiently. Suppliers used the EPOS information as both a demand and a replenishment signal. With the two companies working together, the core business processes of the supplier and Wal-Mart became virtually one core business process.

Many companies guard this information, fearing their competitors will learn from it; Sam Walton did not care what competitors knew, as long as he could maintain relationships with suppliers and have them tend to his customers' needs.

It is interesting to note that Wal-Mart only carries selected brands of items, far fewer than many other discount stores. One reason is that Wal-Mart concentrates on developing "a few good suppliers." Another reason is that some suppliers feel that positioning their brands in Wal-Mart will reflect negatively on their brand image and alienate other retailers because of Wal-Mart's price concessions.

Partly because of this, Wal-Mart was forced to cultivate good suppliers, and has found over time that maintaining close relationships with suppliers is key. And over time many suppliers have become proud to be Wal-Mart suppliers because of these relationships between supplier, retailer, and customer. Today, even suppliers that are very concerned with brand equity, such as Procter & Gamble, have come to realize the advantages of working with a company such as Wal-Mart.

In fact, the relationship between P&G and Wal-Mart has caused P&G to rethink some of its brand management techniques, and could revolutionize the industry. Because Wal-Mart promises customers "always lower prices" it negotiates with suppliers to supply product at always lower prices to Wal-Mart, rather than in the traditional way of offering a variety of trade discounts based on season, volume, and a host of other reasons. Over the time P&G has been working with Wal-Mart, P&G has come to realize the benefit to it of one-price supply, the ability to remove a whole series of brand management processes that revolve around trade discounting. P&G in the early 1990s began to move in this direction with other merchandisers, and a few other companies have also tried it. But the retailing industry has so far been slow to want to make such changes.

This rigorous management of the supply chain allowed Wal-Mart to exploit economies of scale in buying, and to get cost breaks from suppliers by helping suppliers effectively manage their own production and raw material purchases. Consequently, Wal-Mart's cost of sales is lower than the industry in general, enabling the company to offer consistently lower prices to customers and create price and availability as BreakPoints.

Changes in the retailing scene have dramatically repositioned players in the U.S. market, and changes in Europe have been no less profound. Even in Japan, where supermarkets have found their activities particularly restricted, the same patterns are becoming apparent.

There is no better example of the use of process focus to gain competitive advantage than the activities of Tesco and Sainsbury's, the leading players in the U.K. retail environment.

Tesco, like Sainsbury's and Wal-Mart, focuses strongly on the supply chain, making a high investment in systems to automate the entire supply process. In this respect, the company has caught up with, and in some areas surpassed, Sainsbury's, as in applying electronic data interchange (EDI) techniques.

The ability of Tesco to handle supply-chain issues, while at the same time responding rapidly to customer needs, has created new business opportunities, as for example in the innovative idea of being a gasoline supplier. Today, Tesco is among the top four suppliers of gasoline to the U.K. market, tempting customers with fast service and attractive prices.

That Tesco had clear process choices in seeking to compete successfully against the power of Sainsbury's is evident when one considers by contrast another successful retail group, Aldi, a discount grocery, a strong international player. Here the approach to process is very different, relying on minimal computer support and mainly on manual systems, and deliberately limiting the product range to 2000 items so that people can work entirely with manual systems.

The final case worthy of note in the European retail sector is that of textiles and clothing, where both Marks & Spencer in the United Kingdom and Benetton in Italy have in very different ways made strong process thinking a critical part of major business success.

Benetton's formula has been to establish a global franchise operation with very strict standards of control of product, supply, presentation and stocking in stores. By rethinking the manufacturing process so that garments are dyed as the last step in the manufacturing process, Benetton has minimized variation in manufacture and considerably shortened the supply chain.

Further, by making heavy use of information technology, the company has been able to use EPOS information in over 7000 stores worldwide as replenishment orders for manufacturers of products that they have sought to make as uniform as possible worldwide.

At Marks & Spencer, by contrast, all manufacture is done by specially chosen suppliers, supplying stores that are almost exclusively the property of Marks & Spencer. However, Marks & Spencer becomes intimately involved with the manufacturing processes of all its suppliers, so that over the years the company's own labelled products have become highly respected for their quality, capturing a substantial share of the U.K. market and becoming increasingly influential in other countries as well.

As all of these retailers have improved their core business processes, they have been able to use improved capabilities to launch new products, taking advantage of these enhanced capacities. The result in the U.K. market has been an explosion of product offerings in food and groceries that has taken the customer far, far away from the restrictions, and quality limitations experienced by the consumer of 25 years ago. Similar results are discernible in all of the major industrialized countries, thanks to the consumer orientation and innovative, entrepreneurial character of retailing.

The message in this little exercise is quite powerful; that is, no matter which one of the key value metrics a company focuses on as its basis of competition—flexibility for Benetton, robustness for Marks & Spencer, price and delivery reliability through supply chain management for Wal-Mart—the company that reaches the pinnacle of success in achieving its chosen metric is in good position to find and effect a Breakpoint and achieve significant marketplace enhancement, all through a simple focus on the customer.

The business opportunities for reengineering lie in a redefinition of the interface with the customer and in encouraging the customer to expect ever higher standards of service. In some circumstances, even small changes in the way improvements are made or presented to customers will result in breakthrough levels of business performance.

The Japanese auto industry was able to break into the difficult German market, especially the low-cost end, by offering extensive options at the basic cost and superior after-sales service. Since the Japanese enjoyed considerable product-cost advantages, such apparently generous options and service offers were not actually unduly onerous. Yet the perception has allowed the Japanese to take considerable market share. Interestingly, at the same time, the German car makers have taken an important slice of the Japanese auto market—140 000 vehicles per year—of much higher unit value added.

It is safe to say that most companies have scarcely scratched the surface of what is possible when one goes through the logical analysis of customer needs and expectations in an effort to identify opportunities for changes in operational performance.

Competition as Driver

Clearly, competitive pressures drive companies to look at their process and determine that they can become competitive—or even leapfrog the competition—by focusing on process.

The Motorola Company, mentioned in Chapter 1 as a company that came to the notion of Breakpoint deliberately, was forced to seek a Breakpoint because competitors were making pagers at half the price. Motorola needed something to get the market to stop focusing on price, and production of a custom pager in three hours was just the ticket.

In a similar way, IBM in the mid-1980s redesigned the entire process by which it made computer printers by simplifying the process of designing and manufacturing the product, and Xerox did the same with the way it produced photocopy machines.

In many instances, competition goes hand in hand with customer service; the competition is connecting with the customer, so a company needs to define its processes that connect with the customer and subsequently reengineer them.

Cost as Driver

There is little doubt that aside from losing contact with the customer or finding that competitors are connecting with customers better than you are, loss of cost control is the most common cause of difficulty in businesses. One wonders, with all the functional competency in the financial and accounting areas, why companies do fail to keep costs under control.

Some companies simply lose sight of their costs. Others engage in excessive measurement or measurement that is improper for current business conditions. Others are burdened by old-fashioned cost accounting, which spreads indirect costs across all processes so that the true cost of each process or activity is difficult if not impossible to determine. In process-oriented companies, costing must be activity based, so that a true picture can be derived.

Harley-Davidson is an example of what can happen when a company loses control of costs. In the 1960s and 1970s, Harley-Davidson and Indian owned the U.S. motor cycle market. So long as they stayed relatively similar on costs they could compete on style and performance. Consequently, the size and cost of the bikes increased.

Honda and Kawasaki came into the market with significantly lower costs and smaller machine size, but with performance that was similar to the big "hogs" produced by the U.S. competitors. Due in large part to protective tariffs and a Herculean effort at operational improvement (employing the Just-In-Time philosophy of process management), Harley-Davidson survived and prospered; but, alas, Indian is no more.

It is important that Harley-Davidson did not undertake a simple cost-cutting effort, but sought process enhancement through JIT, taking costs out while cutting lead time and becoming more flexible and responsive to the market.

Excessive financial measurements by functional experts in finance and administration who are more concerned with and more adept at keeping score than they are at determining the right score and making sure the company achieves it, can also hurt a company's cost structure.

For instance, when Texas Instruments made the 99A personal computer, it could assemble and test the product in less than four hours. Yet, it took a week to get the computer assembled and tested, because after each operation the cost accounting system required data collection. The system increased inventory and increased exposure to quality problems, since errors were not immediately discovered, while increasing cost as well.

Companies are also prone to use the wrong performance measures, or at least those inappropriate to changing business conditions. For instance, even after the 1973 oil embargo American auto manufacturers were still measuring comfort and styling, rather than miles per gallon.

Costs continually have to be re-addressed so that wastage is kept to a minimum, in terms of both direct and indirect costs while maintaining and even enhancing customer satisfaction. Excess costs feed on themselves, creating further excesses and inefficiencies.

The constant state of war on waste and cost that should exist universally is lacking in many organizations, especially large multi-site operations that have become used to favorable business conditions and found ways to shift or hide costs. In addition, it is no longer appropriate to look for cutting costs and the individual task or activity level as the way to achieve significant cost reduction. Rather, one has to define the total process vision or flow and then attack the costs within the process.

General Motors spent $40 billion on cost reduction and technology improvement through the 1980s, but realized little for its investment because it did not focus on its own processes and the external connections—especially parts suppliers; rather, GM looked first at internal cost reduction through automation of direct labor. It was only in 1992 that GM began to look at having its captive in-house supplier plants compete for its business, and to creating strategic alliances with its parts suppliers either within the GM umbrella or outside.

Thus, for the leading organizations, Business Process Reengineering holds the greatest promise for answering the key question that previous attempts to fight off market or business condition changes have been unable to answer: *How can a company cut costs while at the same time not only maintaining but improving responsiveness to all of its major constituencies, such as customers, suppliers, shareholders, employees, and regulators?*

The way to accomplish this is through questioning the very basic ways in which the organization operates. Only then can a company get a grip on the waste that has come into being throughout the organization gradually and surreptitiously.

Technology as Driver

Even companies that maintain the best customer relations and wage the constant war on waste and costs can find themselves vulnerable to technological shifts and competitors who attack the marketplace through the exploitation of technology, whether applied to the products themselves or to the processes by which they are made. In short, technological shifts force companies to break the china, redefine the state of their industry and their business, and reengineer their core business processes.

Technology is not the focus in this book; although technology and its importance will be recognized throughout the book, rather we will focus on the core business processes and how they might be improved by technological developments.

Enhancements in process technology might be considered a part of cost containment through productivity increases. Indeed, the ruthless and rapid exploitation of new process technology as market share is gained and markets grow is a key characteristic of competitive strategy in technologically sensitive industries. Just look at the cost improvements attainable as progress is made up the learning curve. But it is also important to look at technology breakthroughs in products that bring about a major shift in an industry.

An example is Apple Computer. Apple chose deliberately not to compete on cost or compatibility with the existing suppliers of personal computers and by doing so broke the *de facto* standards set by the IBM PC. Apple did this by breaking the china and creating a new type of computer/user interface— known as the graphical user interface (GUI)—within its Macintosh line of computers that an increasing number of customers found exciting, once they overcame their initial resistance and discomfort at having to un-learn the way they had done things on MS DOS-based systems. (This book was written using Macintosh technology, with various authors at various stages of learning how to use Macintosh.)

In relentlessly pursuing its own direction, Apple has steadily made inroads into the PC computer market while maintaining margins superior to the market as a whole, growing from two men in a garage to $6 billion in market capitalization in less than 15 years.

More important, the Apple "iconic" methodology has become recognized as the preferred interface for many customers, and competitors are either emulating Apple's technology or finding ways to form alliances with Apple; even IBM created the Tagiland alliance with Apple.

It is important to note that the high-cost strategy hurt Apple when Microsoft introduced Windows on to the market, forcing Apple to rethink its strategy and compete on cost. After successfully beating back the low-cost challenge, Apple was able once again to compete on technology excellence with cost parity.

Apple's ability to change the rules of the game mirror those of Digital Equipment Corporation (DEC) two decades earlier, when DEC systematically introduced the concept of mini-computing into the mainframe-dominated world, initially capturing engineering and technical applications, then subsequently attacking the entire gamut of computer operations.

Both Apple and DEC created and sustained a fundamental shift in the computer industry and forced responses from competitors. While technological breakthrough as the way of changing the basis of competition is nothing new—indeed it is the essence of industrialization—what is new is companies deliberately seeking a technological way to break the deadlock in a tough competitive environment and looking to technology as one of the tools to achieve a radical improvement in business performance coincidental with changes in other dimensions.

The key is for a company to build process advantages that allow it to enhance or exploit technology, and to leverage this through such processes as new product development or worldwide market rollout. Also, processes that protect an investment in the critical technology itself are important.

An example is Avions Marcel Dassault in France, which developed a superior capability in computer-aided design. While this started out as a core technology, it was transformed into a core business process, as the company changed its entire way of doing business because of the technological breakthrough. Not wishing to see its technology supplanted by offerings from the competitive giants such as IBM, Dassault licensed its world-beating CATIA system to IBM so that CATIA became an industry standard, thereby helping Dassault itself to preserve leadership and protect its investment in both a critical core process and an enabling technology.

In this case, both Dassault and IBM have redefined their core business process. Dassault realized that to reach its customers the company ought to develop its software on the hardware most customers were familiar with; IBM realized that it could not do all forms of applications software by itself and should form alliances with the best application software developers for particular types of applications.

Similar examples can be found in industries as diverse

as microprocessors, consumer electronics, and automotive components.

The Parker Manufacturing Company broke new technological ground in making hacksaw blades better than anyone else. The company allied itself with Sears to enhance its distribution; Sears insists that any hacksaw manufacturer who makes saws for the Sears label use Parker blades.

The 3M company, which many people still consider as leader in "adhesives," really has over the years created a host of technologies with a common process technology that might be thought of as "putting goop on a substrate." From post-it notes to magnetic tape to sandpaper, the process technology is common, and 3M has continually been able to leapfrog competition or come up with another combination of goop on a substrate over the years. The company's goal is for half of its annual profits to come from products that are less than five years old. By sticking to its process technological base and finding more ways to connect a substrate with a surface substance, 3M spends little of the five-year window debugging new products; the company basically knows that it will work when it goes out the design door.

Shareholders as Drivers

At the senior management level, it is foremost among responsibilities to ensure that the shareholders in the business receive at least an adequate but preferably a better return on their investment.

Needless to say, shareholders are looking for bold, imaginative leaders who can break out of the rather staid, dull and even stagnant ruts into which increasing numbers of companies have fallen, and are increasingly prepared to act strongly in order to see major changes implemented.

In the same way that employees must see early improvements in order to understand the power of a process orientation and in order for them to rally behind it, shareholders too must see some early, incremental improvements before they will sign on for the long term. Figure 2.2 shows this incremental progression.

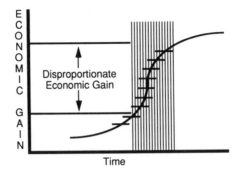

Figure 2.2   *BreakPoint by incremental steps.*

A good example of how shareholder value drives visionary thinking can be seen at Britain's chemical giant ICI. Under the stewardship of Sir John Harvey Jones, ICI became a much leaner organization. Yet, in the early 1990s under its new chairman, Sir Denys Henderson, ICI became the target of an unfriendly takeover bid by Hanson Trust.

Following the Hanson bid and in order to create better shareholder value, ICI leaders created a strategy for operations that could shake the stable world of the giant chemical companies to its core; ICI is breaking up into two components, a biosciences business and a bulk chemicals business. While the biosciences company will gain the advantage of higher price-to-earnings ratios afforded this sector, the bulk chemicals company needs to concentrate on processes that result in low production costs and overheads in order to compete in the cut-throat commodity business of bulk chemicals.

It will be very much a part of the 1990s culture to find people who are visionary and effective in meeting such new demands. The new era will need leaders who are no less adept at the financial legerdemain that has prevailed for the last 20 years, but who combine such skills with the ability to lead an effort to radically reengineer core business processes and business units in order to address the underlying issues.

It is interesting to note that very few, if any, of the CEOs of companies that have been at the forefront of Business Process Reengineering and BreakPoints came from the rather confining background of finance: Andy Guarriello at AT&T

Power Systems was a manufacturing engineer; O'Neill at Alcoa was a lawyer; and Sir John at ICI had been a naval officer and tax inspector.

Politics, Economics, Legislation, and Regulation: a Great Influencer, though not a Driver

While at the microeconomic level it can be argued that through customer satisfaction, cost control, and technological advancement companies can be largely in control of their destiny and able to implement radical change, there is another dimension entirely out of the organization's control: that of politics, economics, legislation, and regulation.

For example, with the rapid collapse in cold war conditions following the breakup of the old communist block, the defense industry worldwide is posed with a considerable problem, how to convert its existing capabilities to alternative uses, create new markets for its military products, or downsize.

On the regulatory front, changes in product standards (i.e. motor vehicle emissions), tighter material-usage specifications (such as chlorofluorocarbons), recycling requirements, worker safety standards, and a host of other issues all have drastic impact on business processes. Companies that can most easily meet these regulatory conditions or even have an impact on creating them—Monsanto, for instance, which aggressively seeks environmental legislation that tightens regulations to levels it already meets or beats—can create Breakpoint competitive advantage, and rewrite the rules of their industry.

It is three–five times more expensive to retrofit environmental controls than it is to reengineer the process in order to eliminate "end of the pipeline" contaminants. To be environmentally proactive and reengineer a clean process, a company *must* challenge its existing processes, rather than fighting the regulation, as many companies are inclined to do. In the United States, litigation costs to industry over environmental matters were over $5 billion in 1991.

3M is meeting the environmental challenge and to date has saved over $500 million by taking a process view of pollution protection.

While environmental issues are foremost, safety issues are also of great concern. Passive restraints in autos—airbags and automatic safety belts—were fought by car companies for years. There were even those who lobbied against regulations for child-safety seats. But some car companies have used strict adherence to safety regulations and legislation as selling points.

In the United States, Chrysler has been out front, advertizing heavily that beginning with the 1992 model year, all cars would have driver-side airbags as standard equipment, and even designing a fold-out child safety seat as standard equipment in its Plymouth Voyager/Dodge Caravan seven-passenger mini-van, a favorite of families with young children.

THE NEED FOR RADICAL CHANGE IS APPARENT

Like an umbrella draped over all of these issues, globalization continues apace, trade barriers throughout Western Europe are being removed, and new markets are being opened as Eastern Europe begins the integration process with the West, and as many Asian and Latin American markets become moderately more prosperous and more consumer oriented.

Companies clearly need to find radically new ways to operate in an increasingly fast-paced, complex and interrelated world. Chief executives must take the necessary steps to set their organizations on the path to higher levels of business performance.

It is clear from working with leading organizations throughout the world that new management paradigms have appeared since the late 1980s as the logical successors to the JIT and TQM philosophies, which so many Western managers acquired from the late 1970s to the late 1980s from Japanese manufacturing companies.

As a result of increased global competition, and made more urgent by a slackening of worldwide demand, visionary CEOs increasingly seek to lead from the front and set new strategies for change to achieve both step improvement in business performance and BreakPoints in the marketplace.

Continuous improvement is simply not good enough in the situation businesses find themselves in today. Although the mentality of quality and continuous improvement is a *necessary* condition, it is not *sufficient* for making the rapid transformations being sought under the influence of a variety of powerful drivers such as cost, quality, regulation, and shareholders.

The ability of an organization to accept, digest and respond to these rapid changes places extreme pressures on leaders and organizational structure and culture. Formal "change management," which is discussed in more detail in a later chapter, is a necessary coincident set of processes that must be undertaken during a Business Process Reengineering effort.

The external environment, the company's strategy and mission, the cultural style and, most importantly, leadership capacity, are the greatest influences in how well an organization will achieve rapid rates of transformation. The entire process is helped by a sense of urgency or crisis, although that is, in fact, the most difficult time to undertake such changes.

Changes will seem chaotic, as companies effectively sweep away bureaucracies and instil a multidisciplinary process-driven approach into their business. But for the change agents in organizations, there will be room to thrive. Their leaders will support them in their efforts and reward and celebrate success. Such process managers are the people who by their effort, adaptability and knowledge, will emerge as the leaders of tomorrow.

When it is necessary to take such large steps it is essential to undertake the tasks knowing the risks involved. Using the core business process approach to change radically can limit and control exposure, as demonstrated throughout the examples in this book.

This can be done in a number of ways.

1   Because it is a core business process, everyone knows more about it than if it were a supporting process. While the risk may be greater if Business Process Reengineering is implemented poorly, the mere fact that everyone knows the detail makes it easier to ellide the functions after careful study. (See Chapter 4 on the Business Process Reengineering approach for more detail.)

2 The order of magnitude is so great that Business Process
   Reengineering cannot be implemented overnight. It must be
   done incrementally. (See chapter 5 on BreakPoints for a
   discussion of mapping speed, quality, cost, and service in
   order to rank-order the implementation steps.)

3 When large management information systems changes are
   conceptually reengineered, it is usually appropriate to
   emulate them with paper and pencil first. In some cases, as
   with the Bank of Boston, the operators found that the
   streamlined process did not require the proposed computer
   system after all.

A CASE STUDY OF RADICAL CHANGE THROUGH ADHERENCE TO A PROCESS FOCUS

Let us take a close look at how the leader of one operating unit
of a major U.S. corporation used visionary thinking to drive his
business to focus on processes and radically improve performance
while forcing competitors to think about the changes his business
made as setting the standards for the basis of competition.

It is important to realize that this is an operating unit discussed
here; as will be discussed in greater detail both in Chapter 5 on
BreakPoints, and in Chapter 8 on organizing and managing for
process orientation, it is at the operating unit level that true Business
Process Reengineering undertakings occur. At the corporate level of
the business the size of AT&T, Asea Brown Boveri, ICI, or the other
global corporations discussed in this book, executive leaders can
only set the right conditions within which operating unit leaders can
strive for rigorous process adherence.

AT&T Power Systems: from Captive to Market Force

In 1988, AT&T created the Power Systems Division, a strategic business unit, headquartered in Dallas. The division, part of the Microelectronics Group, had five operating units and built almost 100
percent custom-designed products, including switching power
supplies (OLS), DC–DC converters, linear power supplies, uninter-
ruptible power supplies (UPS), and other products. The customer
requirements for such products are high quality and long mean time
between failure (MTBF).

The new division found itself losing millions per year, with product costs higher than competitors, lead times of months instead of days, and the time to prototype to a customer request three–four months while the market was increasingly requiring prototype responses in weeks.

Despite the court-ordered breakup of AT&T years earlier, separating the company into an equipment and long-distance service company and a host of autonomous Regional Bell Operating Companies—RBOCs or "Baby Bells"—there were few market drivers in the business, The power systems business ran as if it were still operating as the sole supplier to AT&T final assembly facilities. There was a lack of focus and accountability was unclear. People worked in functional silos, with minimal inter-functional contact and support. There were often multiple "scorecards" for the same tasks, compliance was rewarded and correction of problems by seeking root causes was discouraged.

In 1987, sales of power systems equipment were divided 60 percent to AT&T final assembly divisions; 30 percent to the Baby Bells, many of whom were applying to the court to go into direct competition with AT&T in telephone equipment manufacture; and 10 percent to original equipment manufacturers (OEMs), including computer manufacturers. There was minimal presence in European markets.

Andy Guarriello was named Divisional VP and General Manager. A man with a strong manufacturing background, Guarriello is a natural leader who believes that with guidance and kindness, every member of an organization can be a problem solver, and that if everyone's problem-solving energy is harnessed, an organization can be strengthened immensely.

Guarriello began a continuous improvement effort to "clean up the inside business" and return the business unit back to profitability. Just-In-Time and Total Quality Management were implemented in Dallas; Matamoros, Mexico; and New River, Virginia. The Nashville, Tennessee plant and business were sold.

Redundant layers of management were removed—the organization was "leaned out" as nearly 40 percent of the supervision was eliminated. The old functional organization structure was replaced with job-based units that had a cross-functional structure.

A product marketing group was developed for power systems, instead of sharing marketing and sales with the entire Microelectronics Group.

The design engineering group for power systems that had been located at Bell Laboratories in New Jersey was relocated to the Dallas factory. Almost half of the engineers refused to move, but the key personnel were heavily recruited and many did move.

Moving engineering to the divisional site was of fundamental importance if the division was ever going to break the old AT&T mold and enact real BreakPoint reengineering. Design engineering had always been linked with basic R&D at Bell Laboratories, the research campus in the New Jersey hills, famous as the site of such revolutionary inventions as the transistor. No longer could designers work in isolation, throwing products to the manufacturing facilities. They had to be in the trenches, designing for manufacturability, quality, and quick lead times.

These changes helped deliver savings of $60 million by 1990 and brought the Power Systems Division back to competitive profitability.

During the first six months of the initial effort, Guarriello developed his vision. The division would be a $2 billion business by 1998, more than three times the sales of 1990. It would shift its sales from 60 percent internal to AT&T to 70 percent sales to Baby Bells and OEMs, focusing on the notebook computer and cellular markets.

New products would be designed as "service sets" rather than using the then popular modular approach. Standard "platforms" would be used to provide custom solutions. The division would aggressively look for business in the rapidly privatizing national telecommunications companies throughout Europe and South America that were increasingly adopting the U.S. 48-volt standard.

Finally, Guarriello determined that the Power Systems Division would win the Deming Award for quality by 1994.

The efforts of 1988–90 set the stage for these kinds of bigger changes, and as they occurred Guarriello could see the determination and energy employees at every level were putting into the effort, even though he had not shared the grand vision with them yet.

Both of the major goals, growing a $2 billion annual business and winning the Deming Award, could only be accomplished by breaking the china and building the business anew for a second time. And Guarriello sees both of these accomplishments as being enablers for continued excellence. As the BPR undertaking becomes more mature, he feels that the incremental goals he sets must be higher for employees to continue having the sense that they are making great strides rather than plodding along and falling into an effort that is merely one of continuous improvements.

"People change as breakthroughs happen," Guarriello says. "Initially, they were too busy fighting fires" to have assimilated the major changes necessary to reach the vision. If they thought the vision was unattainable, they might have been discouraged, thinking that their own efforts either were not good enough or that they were on a fool's errand.

With the excess capacity developed through JIT manufacturing, Guarriello consolidated the division's entire North American operations either at Dallas or Matamoros and closed New River. At the same time, a small facility was opened in England to respond to two U.S. customers who required local sourcing for their European operations.

On the design end, Design for Excellence was implemented, reducing design cycle time by 69 percent.

In 1991 Guarriello shared his vision with the entire workforce of the Power Systems Division. He believed he could honestly tell them they had come 50 percent of the way. He could show them how they had changed the culture and achieved breakthroughs, rather than telling them that they must change the culture and achieve breakthroughs. He believed they had the confidence and the determination to see the task through. Guarriello says:

> "People are funny, it seems the more educated they are, the more they think they know, the harder they are to change. Direct reports do it because they must, middle managers demonstrate their resistance by procrastination, and shopfloor people revel in change. The development engineers want recognition, celebrations, the folks on the floor just want you to listen and support their ideas."

In 1992 the Power Systems Division won the Shingo Award for excellence in operations. The drive for the award was not an attempt to increase market share—rather, it was the result of hard work and realizing that a lot had to be done to clean things up in a very short time. There has been a BreakPoint marketplace reaction to the award.

The next steps on the way to the 1996 vision are all BreakPoint oriented. They are:

1 Linking the value chain:
   (a) suppliers–operations–customers;
   (b) customers–design prototype–suppliers–operations.
2 Continuing the quality crusade.
3 Developing new, innovative technologies that are driven by immediate market needs and not by basic research
   in new horizons (which is still the domain of Bell Laboratories in New Jersey).
4 Continuing specific cost-reduction efforts in peripheral areas that were not part of the original efforts.

Now that breakthroughs occur regularly, Guarriello says, "we can begin to place an emphasis on operational excellence as a means to achieving the vision, because everyone in the organization can see the breakthroughs and because they *all* can contribute."

A FINAL WORD

We know from implementing radical change that transform-ation of a business revolves much more around the issues of mission and strategy, leadership style and corporate culture, than it does around transactional issues such as management systems, policies and procedures, or operational practices.

It is also important to have a solid grasp of the true nature of external pressures and competitive performance.

The risks are reduced by being congnizant of these practi-calities, and by focusing on the essentials—the core business processes and the ultimate strategic capabilities that they represent.

Once these simple realities are grasped, the CEO will be confident in his ability to manage transformational change and achieve BreakPoints in performance and customer satisfaction. Armed with this confidence and "can do" spirit, he will not hesitate to apply this new-found power as frequently as his visionary sense shows him the way forward.

3
Understanding Processes

Business Process Reengineering is a systematic approach to radically improving the core business processes and key supporting processes. Discreet improvement of a company's portfolio of products or services, or standalone functions, fails to focus on a company's strategy and therefore cannot lead to radical improvement.

It is important when considering undertaking Business Process Reengineering to understand thoroughly what processes are and why they are key to business success. As well, it is important to understand the three possible reasons for undertaking Business Process Reengineering:

1 cost reduction;
2 renewed competitiveness (parity or best practice);
3 competitive dominance.

WHAT ARE PROCESSES?

A process is a set of linked activities that take an input and transform it to create an output. Ideally, the transformation that occurs in the process should add value to the input and create an output that is more useful and effective to the recipient either upstream or downstream.

There are processes everywhere. Take data, apply rules to organize that data, and you have created information.

broad
sense
word

Processes are the basis on which all manufacturing entities create wealth. Take a piece of metal, cut it, bend it, machine it to create a bracket for a shelf. You have taken an input, transformed it through a series of value-adding activities, and created an output—a piece of metal that is now useful.

Beginning in the early 1980s, Western manufacturing companies set to work feverishly streamlining their operating processes through the use of tactical process orientation tools such as JIT and TQM techniques in order both to enhance the value they add to their manufactured outputs and to reduce the costs of excess inventories, inefficient and ineffective production, and the indirect costs associated with production.

But processes go much further than merely transforming a piece of metal or the application of the tactical process orientation tools within a company's four walls. Theoretically, a process may start at the point where material is separated from the earth, move through a number of transformation steps, through sales and use, and ultimately through recycling into some other useful object.

Thinking of a process in this broadest sense may get some people to think in the future of the "design for reincarnation" concept, where products are designed not only for the marketplace, and for ease of manufacture (design for manufacturability), but for how they will be taken apart and reused.

By thinking about businesses as processes rather than as functions, managers can focus on streamlining processes in order to create more value for less effort rather than focusing on reducing the size of functions in order simply to cut costs. Cost cuts will naturally occur as non-value-adding activities are removed from the processes and as the processes increase in their level of effectiveness.

WHAT TYPES OF BUSINESS PROCESSES ARE THERE AND WHY ARE THEY IMPORTANT?

In terms of pure numbers the majority of activities a business undertakes are part of non-strategic processes. These processes are usually transparent to the market, but if eliminated or streamlined they can still have longer-term implications such as cost effectiveness.

Business Process Reengineering usually concentrates on the few core business processes out of the many processes that go on in any business. A core business process "creates" value by the capabilities it gives the company for competitiveness. Core business processes are valued by the customer, the shareholder or the regulator and are critical to get right. They are required for success in the industry sector in which the company is doing business; they should be those processes that the business's strategy has identified as critical to excell at in order to match or beat the competition.

There are usually between five and eight core business processes in any industry group, and each by definition has a specific effect outside the organization. As shown in Figure 3.1, competitors and customers define the capabilities required for entry or leadership in every industry segment.

Not all core business processes are immediately apparent, and occasionally the actual production of the goods is not at the heart of a core business process. For instance, in the insurance industry, the actuarial work that leads to a balance of competitive premiums for customers and profit after claims for the company is a core business process. In the U.S. defense

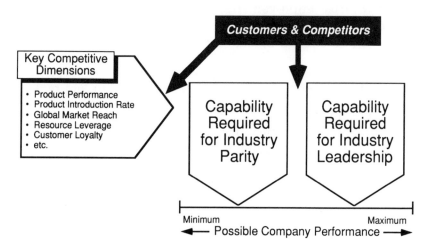

Figure 3.1 *Competitors and customers define the capability required for entry or leadership in every industry segment.*

department contracting industry, alliance management is increasingly a core business process since the DoD has cut back on its funding of R&D, and defense contractors are consolidating their operations; those that remain in the business are increasingly turning to joint R&D, another form of virtuality, instead of competing with each other. In beer brewing, marketing and brand management is a core process.

Business processes, whether core business processes or those that support the core business processes, can be thought of in the same way one thinks of production processes—a set of activities, which can be broken down into tasks, that when taken together take an input, transform it, and produce an output. But while the process of manufacturing is physical, the core business process is more ephemeral—often including the manufacturing process as a component—and connects outside the company.

THREE TYPES OF REENGINEERING: COST, PARITY, BREAKPOINT

There are three types of Business Process Reengineering efforts a company can undertake:

- *Type 1*   Cost improvement
- *Type 2*   To achieve parity, or "best in class"
- *Type 3*   To effect a BreakPoint

A Business Process Reengineering effort can be driven by one of three different business goals, as shown in Figure 3.2.

1 Process improvement can lead to dramatic cost reductions in non-core processes, far beyond what can be accomplished through traditional cost-cutting efforts.
2 Within core business processes, the reengineering effort is usually aimed at reaching "best in class," attaining competitive parity with those who have in the past set the standards and made the rules.
3 The attempt to find and implement BreakPoints, to change the rules and create the new definition of best in class for all others to try to attain.

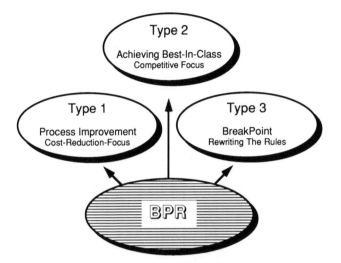

Figure 3.2   *Goals driving Business Process Reengineering.*

It is important for management to look at all of these business goals when determining the direction of a Business Process Reengineering effort, for a number of reasons.

First, not all companies will find BreakPoint opportunities in operations, even if they try; even for those that do, achieving them is another matter.

Second, not all companies will feel it is appropriate to put in the time, effort, and cost of trying to achieve a BreakPoint.

And third, as much as this book focuses on BreakPoints as the ultimate goal, there are almost always opportunities for cost reduction in improving non-core processes, and usually big opportunities to increase competitiveness by improving core business processes.

Type 1   Cost Improvement

Dun & Bradstreet: An Example of Process Improvement

Dun & Bradstreet, the business information provider, was concerned about its customer interface and the means by which credit-rating contracts were established. The processes by which customers signed up to receive Dun & Bradstreet services were well tested, but

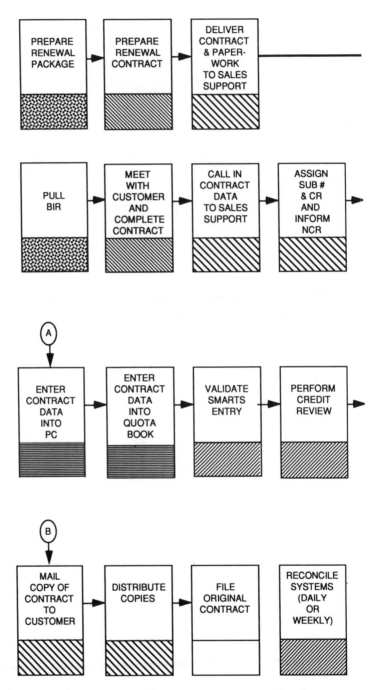

Figure 3.3 *Contract processing—current representative flow.*

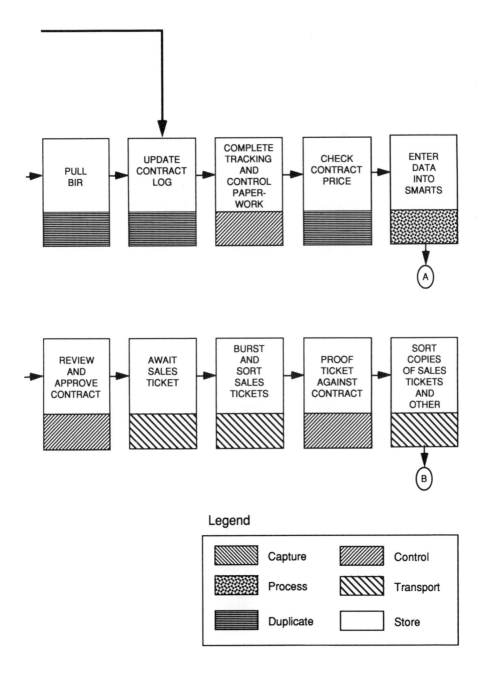

slow, and D&B felt that by reengineering those processes it could achieve significant cost reduction while improving customer service.

Under the eye of top management, analysis of the business processes involved revealed substantial opportunities to enhance the effectiveness of the customer interface so that customer contracts and services could be undertaken in much less time.

Three separate process flows for different contract types were replaced by a single, flexible process flow. The average time to process a contract was reduced from more than a week to less than one day, and 95 percent of customer inquiries can now be resolved while the customer is on the telephone.

Figure 3.3 shows the original contract processing process map for the Dun & Bradstreet company. An analysis of this process showed that over 18 percent of salary and benefits spent at the local-office level ($11.8 million), was spent on contract management. Of that, over two-thirds was spent on duplicating, storing, transporting, and controlling the data.

The process caused unnecessary delays and redundancies. The multiplicity of forms and logs used in the process led to excessive duplication of data, which increased costs. Dependency on manual systems and stand-alone PCs resulted in high control and reconciliation costs. Thirty-seven separate information transfers increased the possibility for error.

In addition to the issues within the process itself, end-of-month submissions for most contracts caused bottlenecks, and annual contract renewal led to additional costs.

While the contract was "in process" for about six business days (2742 minutes), it was actually being worked on for about four hours (220 minutes), with the rest of the time spent "waiting." This means that only about 8 percent of the time the contract is in process is value-added time.

Of the 220 minutes of value-added time, only about 53 minutes were actually devoted to capturing and processing the information necessary to create the contract; the rest was spent on controlling, transporting, duplicating, and storing the information. Given that the $11.8 million the process cost was taken up by salary costs, only $2.8 million was actually being spent on value-added time, the rest of the staff time—$8 million worth—was taken up by controlling, transporting, and duplicating information.

An analysis of the process efforts to simplify, reduce duplicate systems, and eliminate the separate renewal process showed that over $7 million could be saved by using a single, flexible system for contract administration. Figures 3.4, 3.5, and 3.6 show the process steps eliminated in each of these improvements.

Some of the simplification steps for new accounts involve "prework" such as providing new-customer representatives with credit ratings and subscriber numbers before they make sales calls. Others involve "empowerment," of the processing staff, allowing them to approve contracts up to $5000, eliminating multiple approvals. Some involve removing logs, forms, and duplicate data bases.

Figure 3.7 shows the six steps that make up the final process.

The total savings by taking these steps amount to more than $7 million annually, with a reduction of over 200 staff positions, and a modest cost for new technology.

Type 2   Seeking Parity—Moving Toward BreakPoint

AT&T Power Systems Design For Excellence

This example shows how reengineering can bring a business to a position of parity on most aspects of its operations, but with an advantage that, while not a true BreakPoint, can help create a profitable business, retain or gain market share, and allow the business to seek true BreakPoints in other aspects of its product line.

The AT&T Power Systems business unit, located in Dallas, Texas, produces six different product categories, one of which is Custom switching power supplies (OLS). Although this is the product group that produces the smallest revenue, it is a "cost of doing business".

In 1989 AT&T Power Systems found itself in the following competitive position within the OLS business. On the downside:

- a rapidly maturing market, destined to decline in the near future;
- OEM market share pitifully low, but short-term market growth as a medium potential;
- sales effectiveness extremely low, due in large part to the perceived "unsalability" of the product by the sales force;
- costs high relative to competitors.

However, on the upside, the company enjoyed:

- market parity on mean time between failure (MTBF);
- excellent technological capabilities;
- market perception of AT&T quality.

A detailed analysis showed that the product would never be competitive on cost. Even if costs were slashed 31 percent—which

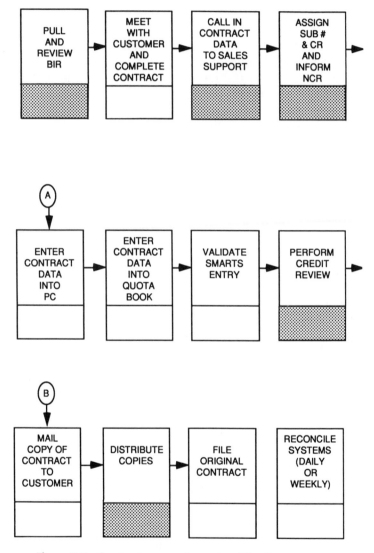

Figure 3.4   *Contract processing—simplification.*

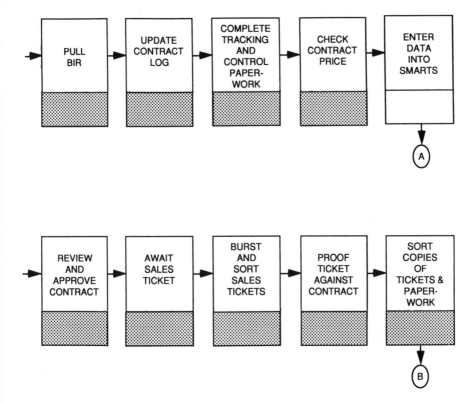

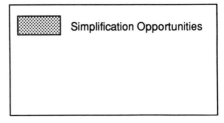

Legend

▒▒▒	Simplification Opportunities

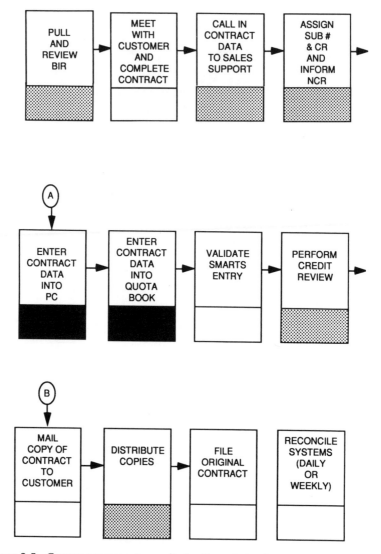

Figure 3.5 *Contract processing—elimination of duplicate systems.*

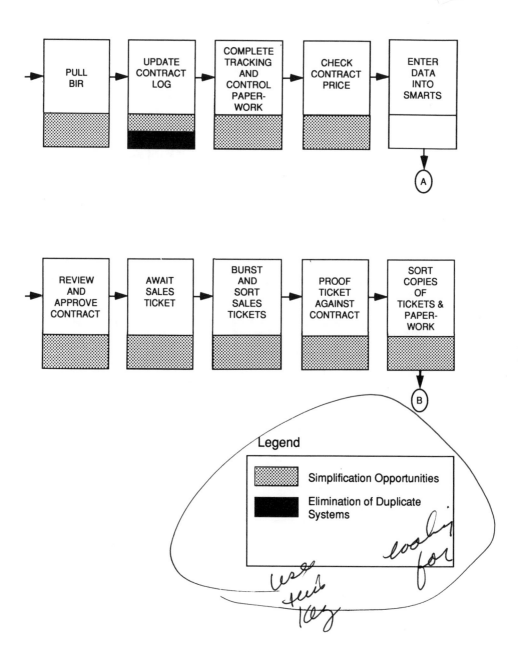

PULL BIR → UPDATE CONTRACT LOG → COMPLETE TRACKING AND CONTROL PAPER-WORK → CHECK CONTRACT PRICE → ENTER DATA INTO SMARTS → A

REVIEW AND APPROVE CONTRACT → AWAIT SALES TICKET → BURST AND SORT SALES TICKETS → PROOF TICKET AGAINST CONTRACT → SORT COPIES OF TICKETS & PAPER-WORK → B

Legend

Simplification Opportunities

Elimination of Duplicate Systems

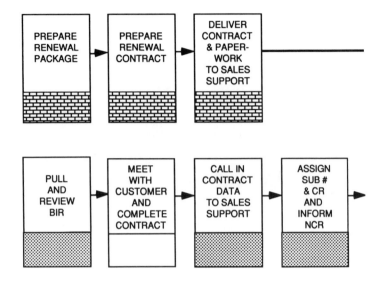

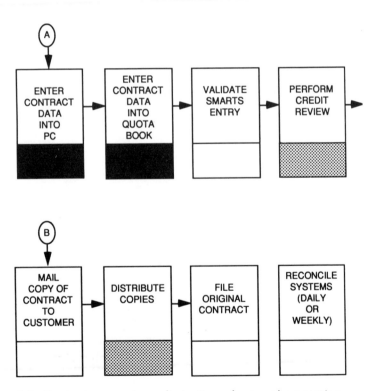

Figure 3.6   Contract processing—elimination of renewal processing.

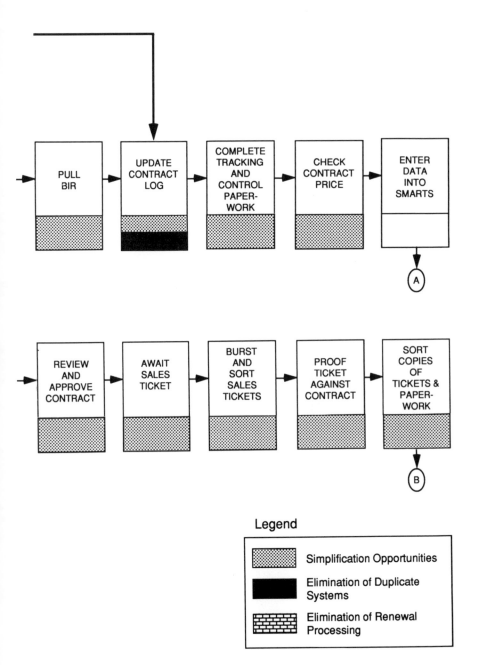

Legend

░░░	Simplification Opportunities
▓▓▓	Elimination of Duplicate Systems
▦▦▦	Elimination of Renewal Processing

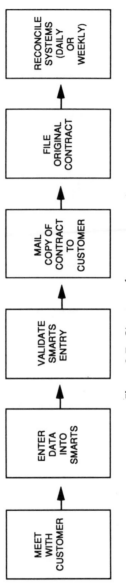

Figure 3.7 *Six steps for new accounts.*

the analysis showed to be possible with aggressive reengineering—and if revenues doubled, the product would still only be in a position of cost parity. But if time for custom prototyping was reduced from the average of 53 days to 5 days, the market would probably forgive the high cost.

It was reasoned that short prototyping turnaround, perceived quality and name recognition, and parity on real quality metrics (MTBF) would offset cost disadvantage and at least grant AT&T's OLS product sustainable market share.

But the breakthrough had to occur relatively quickly, since the losses incurred by the OLS products represented a 66 percent swing in the operating profit of the business unit.

The formally designed process (Figure 3.8) had 42 hand-offs and/or tasks to be performed and 12 scheduled meetings. But when the actual process was mapped, there were *double* the number of both hand-offs and meetings. Under these circumstances, it is remarkable the prototyping process took only 53 days.

The conceptual design of the new process emphasized standard platforms for unique solutions and a dedicated, multifunctional design team. The new process, Figure 3.9, would have 17 hand-offs and/or activities, and only one formal meeting. Analysis showed that the new process would meet the five-day goal for prototyping.

By standardizing the platforms, the design team could be assured of parts availability, since the components were required for other standard subassemblies. The bare printed circuit board was not always optimally configured; but neither speed nor minimal bare board cost was the design driver. And by keeping board design reasonably consistent, there was a significant reduction in time for the development of insertion machine software.

Within the new process, a number of activities from the old process are retained but assigned to a design cell, a group that works in close harmony to cut throughput time. Figure 3.10 shows the steps within the design cell, all of which can be accomplished in a matter of hours, with no real hand-offs. The cell has a set of internal metrics, shown in Figure 3.11.

Each design cell consists of eight and one-half full-time equivalent professionals:

- two electrical engineers, each with a sub-specialty;
- one mechanical/manufacturing engineer;
- one test/software engineer;
- one-half engineer responsible for safety/qualifications testing/ agency approval;

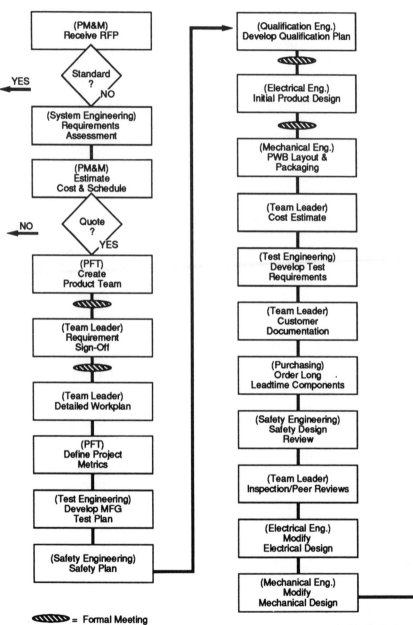

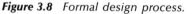 = Formal Meeting

Figure 3.8 *Formal design process.*

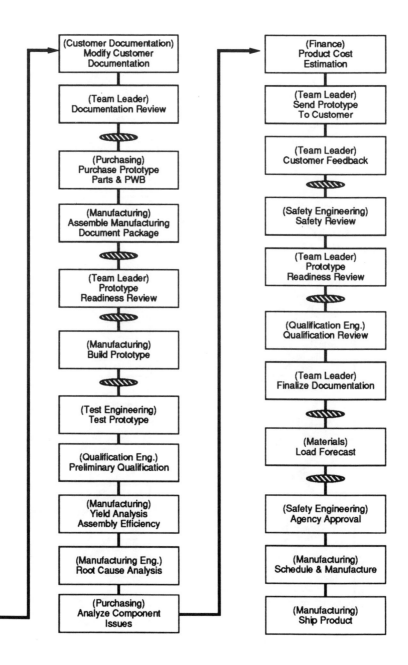

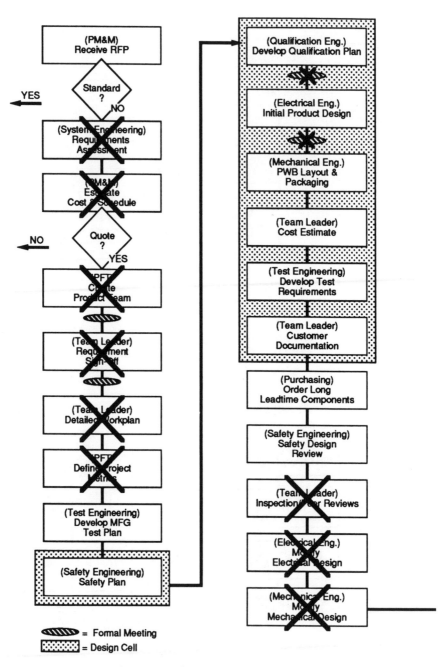

Figure 3.9 *The new design process.*

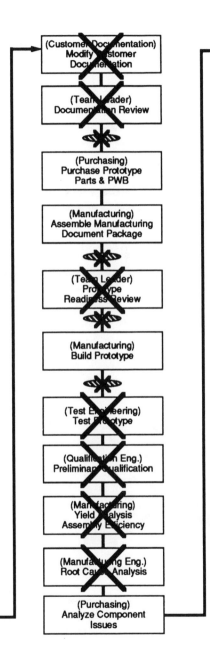

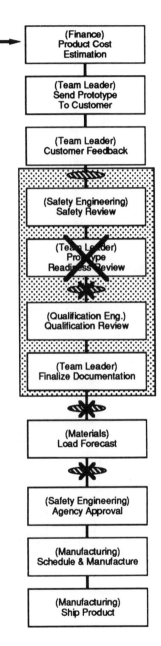

After

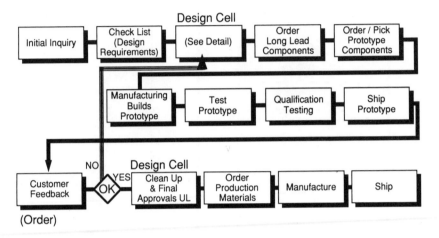

Figure 3.10   *Steps in the design cell.*

Design Cell

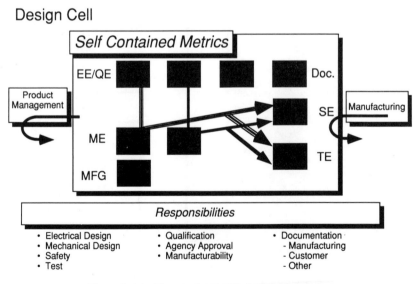

Figure 3.11   *The design cell's internal metrics.*

- one quality engineer;
- one model builder;
- one project manager.

Each team member takes care of his or her own documentation, rather than passing it all off to the technical writer; the technical writer can then back check the documentation after the fact and edit for clarity.

The key to the design-for-excellence concept's success is that the team members actually work together in the same bullpen, and follow the prototype from the original customer request until the sample is approved by the customer. Hand-off to production is assured to be smooth, since it is the responsibility of all but the four design engineers.

The team is evaluated equally by its speed, proposal success ratio, and subsequent ease of production ramp up. By the end of 1992, the new process was working quite well by these metrics, and the OLS business was becoming competitive.

Type 3   Searching Core Processes for BreakPoints

There is a third kind of business process, the BreakPoint business process, a key set of activities that when carried out in concert drive a key aspect of the business with the goal of dominating the competition. These often spring from the current core business processes within an industry segment, but create a newly defined set of activities that creates a new set of competitive dimensions in an industry, thereby defining the next generation of core processes and imposing these processes on the competition.

For example, in the semiconductor industry, new-product development has always been a core business process. But with the ability one company found within itself to reduce lead times from 16 weeks to four days (lead time being defined as starting with order entry, and the factory process starting with wafer prep), a new competitive dimension was established. Did this negate the need to develop new products? Of course not, but suddenly the market focused on another dimension and customers saw that they could get real benefits without new technology.

Another example is the old Eastern Airlines shuttle from Boston or Washington D.C. to New York and back again. In the 1970s when Eastern created the every-hour-on-the-hour flights, they rewrote the rules of airline travel in the most heavily travelled corridor in the United States. The airline used the same activities and same core competencies, but created a new process that used such innovations as on-board ticketing, one price, and a guaranteed seat, even if the company had to "wheel out another plane just for one customer" to provide a never-heard-of level of service.

Creating new competitive dimensions in an industry does not come without some risk and requires extensive analysis to minimize this risk. None the less the effort can be rewarding. Reengineering the supply chain in the soft drinks industry to achieve BreakPoints in cycle time, service and cost resulted in significant and sustainable competitive advantage for Coca-Cola & Schweppes Beverages Limited (CC&SB).

Coca-Cola and Schweppes—BreakPoints in the Supply Chain

CC&SB is a joint venture in Great Britain between Cadbury Schweppes, the U.K.'s number one producer of mixers, and Coca-Cola, the country's number one producer of cola.

As the joint venture's managing director, Derek Williams, said, "CC&SB decided that a full merger was the wrong course to pursue and that what they had to do was to build a new company."

When the two companies joined forces, a large increase in sales volume for the two brand lines was realized, which became the catalyst for an urgent review of capacity. The apparent need for substantial investment was the trigger for a complete reappraisal of the core business process of manufacturing and supplying soft drinks throughout Britain.

Williams had been managing director of Schweppes for some time before the joint venture was launched. With a background in personnel, Williams is widely acknowledged as a highly effective team builder. Two other top executives who oversaw the reengineering effort were Peter White, the operations director, an astute logistics professional, and John Turner, the manufacturing director, a visionary engineer.

The operations study needed to be conducted quickly; at the same time it needed to be comprehensive and lay out a vision for the next 10–15 years. CC&SB's manufacturing plants produce a variety of canned, bottled and packaged products. The manufacturing facilities were clearly going to be central to any new approach to operations.

Two teams were established to do the analysis. One modeled the core business processes of manufacture and distribution, while the other investigated the effects of changing external influences such as legislation and market forces on the economics of the business.

At the time, one of the fastest canning lines in the world was running in the CC&SB plant in Milton Keynes; 2000 cans per minute. The challenge was to use this new technology not only to provide sufficient capacity to meet demand, but also to create a competitive leap forward.

The limiting factor in the filling process, because of size and the effect of gravity on the filling line, is the carrousel filler itself. The availability of high-speed fillers was limited at the time to a few suppliers. The CC&SB team looked at this technology and considered how they might use it to enhance productivity and increase flexibility. The team decided to run two carrousels back-to-back on one line—doubling the effective line speed to 4000 cans per minute.

In this way, the first BreakPoint was found—a 50 percent cut in cycle time per line crew, with little more space needed than for a traditional line, and some investment savings.

If necessary, only one filler can be used, allowing the manning level to be constant while flexing production up or down.

Soon another bottleneck appeared. While it was possible to change over the filling line from one flavor to another relatively quickly, it took up to two hours to change over the packaging line. This negated the advantage of higher filling line speed, and cost flexibility.

Again, process modeling came to the rescue and helped to identify a new packaging machine layout that would enable CC&SB to capitalize on the increased filling line speed and achieve the cycle time BreakPoint.

In the East Kilbride plant, CC&SB had another technologically advanced concept in use. In contrast to accepted practice, Kilbride was actually blowing polyethylene terephthalate (PET) bottles in line rather than using an external bottle supplier. This yielded huge savings in space, since empty PET bottles have a very high volume-to-weight ratio, and are difficult and expensive to handle. The experience from the existing plant drove the decision to use this concept again as a foundation for any new facility.

A deep understanding of the new materials supply, manufacturing and distribution processes began to evolve through the use of process models of the new infrastructure. Trade-offs were evaluated to seek the economic impact of flexibility on the lines versus the lower cost of dedicated equipment. Inventory levels were examined to find the trade-offs between storage space and the cost of capital to increase capacity in the plants to deal with the surges in demand.

The challenge was to cover the increased demand for soft drinks in the hot summer months. A heat wave could create peak demand within hours. But was it realistic to build the plant to cover this demand, since it only occurred infrequently? Failure to satisfy peak demand, however, means loss of profitable growth.

The analysis was complex. "Best Before Date" coding made stock rotation a necessity and moving goods into and out of stock adds to costs and overheads. The CC&SB team realized that the company needed an innovation; a way to get around holding stock for peak demand while not overbuilding capacity just for the three or four few-day periods each summer when peak demand would hit.

A capacity utilization strategy set the high-speed lines running at full capacity seven days a week, and the other lines running at varying capacity in order to flex to demand. During potential peak demand period, the high speed lines run only the most highly desired flavors, only in 33 cl cans, saving changeover and maximizing output.

Here was a second BreakPoint, in the service area. Peak summer demand can now be met without the costs of holding excess inventory, rotating stock that goes beyond "Best Before" date, or increasing the complexity of systems. Customers would always be able to get CC&SB products in a heat wave.

The process models were then used to demonstrate the effect of the type and number of factories on manufacturing and primary distribution costs. These investigations required the consideration of focused versus multipurpose factories, and the number and scale of plants that would be required. All of the options required a fundamental rethinking of operating skills.

Consideration of operating skills led to proposals to increase the level of skills across the staff. It was proposed that line teams should carry out multiple functions, covering inspection, routine main-tenance, hygiene, quality, and machine operations. These proposals were projected to result in line efficiency improvements of more than 85 percent, and to further reenforce the capacity and cost BreakPoints.

One process model examined suggested further stretching of the existing infrastructure. It became clear that in this case, most filling lines would need replacing in the following 15 years, and there may well have to be new plants built. The existing plants were seen as sub-optimal for the then forecast increases in demand, and new sites were evaluated.

The supply and distribution process models showed that if new capacity were to be built that "virtuality" could be exploited if a can-making factory could be built next to the filling plant.

Here was the third BreakPoint, in product cost, which could be achieved by a radical reduction in the working capital needed. No can inventory was required, cans could be supplied as needed and finished goods dispatched directly from manufacturing on trucks to the trade and multiples.

These process-based evaluations of distribution and site acquisition costs by the CC&SB teams of a series of potential sites led to the construction of a major new factory at Wakefield in the North of England. The total contract for both can and PET filling lines was placed with a sole supplier as CC&SB wanted only one contractor, and common equipment in the production area.

It was also decided, after approaching several suppliers, that a can-making plant would be established alongside the new filling factory, with cans supplied to the filling line via a "hole in the wall" operation.

In this way, three BreakPoints—in cycle time, service, and cost—have been effected. As luck would have it, the two summers following the completion of the new factory both had many days of superb weather, with peak demand frequently reached. The production and distribution strategies proved their worth, and CC&SB achieved remarkable performance in the highly competitive cola and soft drinks market in Great Britain.

4
Putting the China Back Together

The kind of radical improvement described in Chapter 3, be it an improvement in a core business process that brings a company to the level of "best practice" or a BreakPoint, will be the outcome of a rigorous effort by a company radically to redesign its business processes.

This effort follows the basic outline of the approach described in this chapter, although each organization must be flexible enough to deal with the particulars it encounters. For companies that wish to search for and effect BreakPoints, the approach must be modified as described in Chapter 5.

The basic Business Process Reengineering approach consists of three phases, as shown in Figure 4.1.

- *Phase 1 Discover*, the phase during which the company creates a strategic vision for dominance or renewed competitiveness in the marketplace, and determines what can be done to its processes to help achieve that strategy.
- *Phase 2 Redesign*, during which the reengineering process is detailed, planned, and engineered.
- *Phase 3 Realize*, implementation of the redesign to effect the strategy.

The Steps Within These Phases Are:

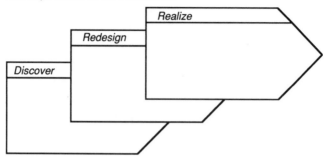

Figure 4.1   *BreakPoint Framework.*

PHASE 1   DISCOVER—A STRATEGIC PLAN FOR DOMINANCE

The Discover phase is essentially an examination of the business that is intended to identify the opportunity and scale for core business process reengineering, with or without seeking BreakPoints.

Much of the activity in this phase has been discussed in earlier chapters; but it is necessary to lay it out in sequence, so as to be able to understand the logic flow, and how the activities within the Discover phase fit into the entire framework.

There are four steps in this phase, as shown in Figure 4.2.

At the beginning of this phase, company management must select the process in which it will conduct its reengineering from among competing opportunities. A multifunctional, multidisciplined team is formed to carry out the effort, and a decision is made as to what tools and techniques will be used from the tool chests of process mapping, analysis, and gathering the voice of the customer.

For instance, the A.C. Nielsen Company is a market research firm that is the only pan-European provider of market information to producers of fast-moving consumer goods. Nielsen captures data about consumer purchases via both in-store collection and its household panels. Nielsen knew that its

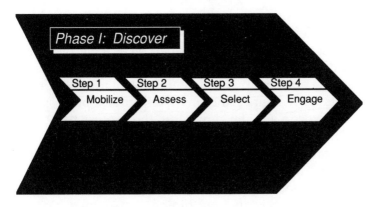

Figure 4.2 *BreakPoint Framework: steps within phase 1.*

customer satisfaction could be a lot better; in an industry where speed and accuracy is important and information changes rapidly, it had the potential to lose market share to more flexible companies in the countries where competition was springing up.

The company decided to undertake a Business Process Reengineering effort in the U.K. and French companies in order to acquire information and disseminate it to customers in a more effective manner. Preliminary work in both the U.K. and French operations showed that there were significant opportunities to improve some of the core in-store audit, production, and client servicing processes, with benefits for customers.

Nielsen found that the subjective customer satisfaction level is the key basis of competition. In order to increase customer satisfaction, it was necessary to find ways to acquire, process, and distribute information it sells in a more accurate, timely, and efficient way.

The key to the Discover phase is confirming the company's strategy. Considerable effort is often put in upfront obtaining a clear understanding of what drives competitive advantage in a particular industry; the industry's value chain and the basis for competition, and how a particular company seeks to gain competitive advantage.

During the Discover phase the processes need to be mapped for the first time, using a technique known as "quickmapping." The quickmap is a first-cut representation of the processes that will need to be refined as the effort progresses. In this first mapping, one defines the external connections, and gives a high-level definition of core business processes and key supporting processes. The quickmap takes a big picture of the process in a macro sense, bounds it, and lays it out. In a simple process, the quick map gives enough detail to begin the search for targets for reengineering; in more complex processes, there is a need to drop very far down into the process before a likely target for the reengineering effort is found.

For instance, in the core business process of designing and rolling out a new automobile, it may be necessary to drive to the level of, say, engine design, or even receiving a casting for an engine block and machining that engine block, then delivering it to the next section of the engine manufacture process, before one gets to a manageable effort.

For example, in the late 1980s a leading automotive company sought a way to increase production of one of its models and increase market share in the growing small-car market in Europe. It was determined that the first constraint in the process was at the engine production line at one of the company's many European manufacturing sites.

As a result the company decided that it needed to carry out a detailed investigation of the machining of engine blocks at the plant to obtain a sustained higher jobs-per-hour rate. This necessitated an analysis of the block machining process, including its relationship to its casting suppliers, in order to increase engine production and therefore overall car pro- duction. The first part of the solution was fixing a mismatch between the castings that came from the supplier and the first machine in the boring process by respecifying the alignment and tightening the weight tolerance for castings, in order to reduce the stress on the machines trying to handle castings of different weights.

The work undertaken successfully at this particular plant helped solve the company's dilemma in delivering more vehicles to the hungry small-car market. It showed how decomposing a huge process into many smaller, manageable processes, and then rethinking one, can have a significant impact on the entire process, both functionally and as a learning experience.

The current business performance needs to be appraised in

order to assure that no major problems are overlooked. This exercise also helps find short-term improvements that can help fund longer-term efforts, or things that need to be fixed right away to plug holes in operations, and helps set up "buy-in" from current functional heads.

Since organizational change will be necessary to align business process and business performance changes, it is necessary to assess the current culture in order to understand the company's need for, readiness, and capability for change. The company needs to think about its cultural norms and determine the proper ways of working, then take advantage of positive forces in the culture while looking at cultural barriers. While it is not time to put into place rigorous change management efforts, it is time to think explicitly about how organizational change can occur.

The company decides on the core business process to change, and the targets for improvement in the other processes. This decision is driven by the high-level vision developed by the corporate or business-unit leader as to "where we'd like to be" at some point in the future, and what core business processes are the key drivers that, when reengineered, can get the company there.

For Nielsen, it was better linking of the data all the way through the process, from POS data capture to new technology in house, to fast and direct transmission to customers. Solutions involved getting POS and household survey data earlier, and processing any late data faster.

There are a number of tools to use to filter out these high payoff process improvements from the original quickmap. These include such internal evaluations as value-added analysis, a first-level quality function deployment, profitability analysis, and marginal costing. In addition, the company needs to look outside the company in order to get the voice of the customer, and might also conduct some benchmarking of best practices in its industry and across industries.

It is necessary to balance the order of magnitude—radical, not incremental, change—against the level of difficulty in carrying out the change. How to assess the "gimme's" vs. the "reaches" will be discussed in detail in Chapter 5 on Break-Points. This is the point at which the company begins truly to "break the china," and looks to create the right atmosphere in which to carry out innovative, radical change.

It is also necessary to continue identifying short-term opportunities in order to fund the longer-term efforts, while making sure not to spend an inordinate amount of time on the short-term opportunities that will be fixed anyway in the course of the more far reaching reengineering efforts.

Even where top management has championed the effort, the effort must be reassessed at this point, and management commitment to undertake the effort that will be necessary to accomplish long-term reengineering for radical change needs to be reconfirmed.

ONE COMPANY'S TRIP THROUGH REENGINEERING— THE COUPLINGS COMPANY

The Company Discovers

Let us take a look at how one company, a manufacturer of specialty couplings, created a successful Business Process Reengineering effort.

The company in question designs and manufactures specialty couplings and spindles. Revenues are approximately $45 million annually.

Located in New York State, the company draws on a labor pool that tends to be relatively unsophisticated and extremely stable. Because it is the largest employer in a small city, stature within the company is perceived to be of greater importance than other more tangible benefits such as salary.

Promotions tended to be from within the same department. Consequently, methodology within departments was self-perpetuating. Departmental responsibilities were clearly established, to a point of near fiefdoms. Change came slowly.

Each item sold is unique to its end use—a true job shop or one-off producer. Every item must be specially engineered. There is, however, significant similarity from one unit to the next. They are all round, with gears and shafts; the major differences are size, gear tooth position and pitch, and number of assembly components.

Order volume was about equally split between OEM (manufacturers of steel drawing mills) and replacement orders from the steel mills themselves. Unit costs were usually in excess of $75 000.

The OEM market was difficult to service because of constant changes in specifications mandated by either the mill designers or by the ultimate customer (the steel manufacturer). The other market was equally difficult, since the high cost mandated that maintenance, repair, and operating supplies (MRO) inventory be carefully monitored by the end user. There was also growing pressure for consignment inventory.

Industry lead time was 32 weeks, with a premium charge for less than that standard if the market could tolerate the rate. There were three manufacturers in the United States, each with about equal market share.

As best could be determined from benchmarking studies, competitors all had similar cost structures. Therefore, when anyone's backlog began to shrink, aggressive cost cutting was promoted throughout the industry, to the point where "at-cost" bids were entered when the market was especially slow. There seemed to be no brand loyalty, even for replacements; assuming delivery could be assured within the 32-week standard, the choice of supplier was completely cost driven, except in emergencies.

Technological advances were selling points, but not determining factors in the replacement market. And although the OEM buyer required responsiveness, he too was more influenced by price because the mills were usually bid firm and he was under budget constraints.

Into this scenario came a new president, with a background in sales and marketing for consumer machinery (lawnmowers and garden tractors). He admitted to knowing little about manufacturing and next to nothing about a job shop environment.

The new president was greeted with the following operating conditions:

- Return on net assets = 16 percent
- Inventory = 19 weeks' raw materials (2.7 turns)
     = 6 weeks in process   (8.7 turns)
- Delivery reliability = 61 percent +/- 5 days
     = 88 percent within 20 days
- Backlog = 17 weeks full
     = 41 equivalent weeks booked
- Capacity available = 56 percent (estimated)
- Incentive payments of 181 percent, or an average of five hours on a standard day, a clear indication of an incentive system with loose standards and an unofficial cap on earnings; both symptoms normally associated with low productivity.

The company was projecting a loss of $380 000 for the remaining eight months of the fiscal year. Industry trends suggested that a 15–20 percent downturn in sales was inevitable. Inside the company, indirect labor had come to be grossly inflated in comparison with direct labor, with a ratio of 2.7 : 1.

While company managers considered these numbers not uncommon for job shops in the industry's environment, coming from a consumer goods background, the new president was aghast. He had his own mental benchmark that emphasized product differentiation, significantly better asset management, higher productivity, and customer service approaching 95 percent.

The president saw a number of opportunities for near-term improvement:

- Morale, especially desire for improvement.
- Improved return on net assets (RONA) via better capacity utilization and working capital reduction.
- Higher productivity via incentive system revision.
- Cost improvements via indirect labor reduction and/or productivity improvement.

For the longer term, he set Breakpoint goals of absorbing underutilized capacity via added volume through market differentiation. He hypothesized that the primary means to gain this differentiation was to offer and realize significant improvements in lead time.

His vision was eight weeks from the customer order being received to delivery of the final product to the customer. His quickmap indicated that it currently took six weeks to manufacture something. With over 50 percent unused capacity it could be done in three weeks, which would allow five weeks for order entry, engineering and procurement. (More detailed analysis revealed that the entire process of order entry to ship could actually be done in six weeks.)

The president ordered a thorough operational review, which confirmed most of his early hypotheses. Raw material inventory was disproportionately large. The average actual lead time was 27 weeks, and direct labor was fully productive only 47 percent of the day. Indirect labor in both the factory and the office were equally as nonproductive as direct labor and strictly departmentalized.

There were bottlenecks at the newer, "more efficient" equipment, while older machinery capable of the same function was rarely used. There was no evidence of procedures, and most guidelines were no more than rules of thumb that had become canonized over years of never being challenged.

Design engineering was neatly compartmentalized into small, medium, and large products, causing queues to become unbalanced to available resources. Even within engineering groups, there were imbalances between design and drafting.

While these problems were easily identified, there were also a host of operations that were commendable and created a firm base on which to reengineer the organization.

- Almost every employee had years of experience and vast knowledge of the product.
- The engineering and cost development records were extensive and easily accessible.
- It was considered an honor to be asked to work overtime for the company, and there was fierce company loyalty.
- The purchasing group was unusually young, eager to learn new techniques, and had already initiated a cost reduction program that had achieved net improvements of 1 percent in real terms or better for three straight years.
- An aggressive quality improvement effort had recently reduced scrap and rework from 4 percent to 0.3 percent through failsafing, especially in engineering.
- The sales department was championing improvements.
- The majority of the lead time consumed was upfront, in the office, as was more than half of the indirect labor.

The union (International Association of Machinists) that represented both the factory floor and the office realized that the company was in for some highly competitive times and union leaders were willing to work toward improvements that would assure the company's viability, so long as they were informed of objectives and planning well in advance of implementation.

Key Issues in Phase 1

There are three key decisions that must be made at the beginning of this phase.

First, it is necessary to determine the approach to core business process modelling that will be used. The arguments for and against great detail in process analysis have been debated over many years. On the positive side, going into great detail allows the team to check the solutions against the known performance of the business, insuring that the model and any

abilities inherent in the design of any physical product. In modern design management, it has been found appropriate to manage many of the development tasks in parallel (called simultaneous engineering) since this dramatically reduces bureaucracy and lead time.

The five steps in this phase are shown in Figure 4.3.

The project team should be confirmed, or modified as needed to carry out a larger, more far-reaching effort. The team then needs to plan this effort. The team may want to add some members with more creativity in process design skills, and may want to add some members with more organizational authority to add authority to the project.

The team needs to undertake a rather rigorous process mapping exercise of the processes to be redesigned—in most instances, a rather straightforward activity-based mapping technique such as those seen in the Chapter 3 examples of Dun & Bradstreet and AT&T Power Systems. In a few instances, either because of the complexity of the particular process, the need to show the process as dynamic rather than static, or because of the culture of the organization, it is necessary to undertake a more rigorous mapping technique (the Appendix, pp. 209–234, shows some of those techniques).

In all cases, however, the goal of the reengineering undertaking is to simplify the process to such an extent that the reengineered process can be mapped using a simple activity-based mapping technique; if a complex mapping technique is

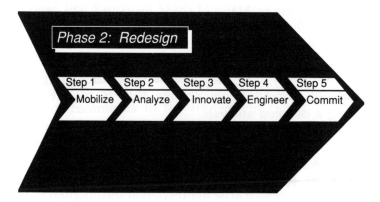

Figure 4.3 *BreakPoint Framework: steps within phase 2.*

necessary to describe the reengineered process, the reengineering effort has not been a success.

At this point, a more detailed vision, or conceptual design of what the core business process will look like after reengineering, needs to be worked out. Analysis of supplier relations, customer relations, and operational processes is performed.

The step from a vision to a solution is not merely a mental leap, but a process that uses tools of innovation and creativity to build a bridge from blue-sky vision to realistic conceptual design.

This is where management needs to challenge all assumptions, principles, and purposes in the way the business runs. Reebok challenged the very foundation of the shoe industry by asking: "why do we manufacture?" Today, the company merely designs and markets, all manufacturing is subcontracted. A major computer hardware company challenged one of its foundations when it asked itself "why do we design low-end models?" Today, it doesn't.

After the vision begets a conceptual design, it must be engineered in a detailed way. How will the company go from as it is now to a process-oriented company, to one that is even more process oriented, and finally to a totally process-oriented company? The change management issues need to be addressed at this point, the barriers need to be acknowledged, and strategies devised to overcome them.

Finally, once again, top management needs to recommit formally to the undertaking.

Let us turn once again to the couplings company to see how it dealt with these issues.

The Couplings Company's Game Plan

The decision was made to address the long-range strategic objective of reducing lead time and generating more volume right away. To do this, the place to start was at the pre-manufacturing activities in the office, where there was significant opportunity for headcount reduction as well as lead-time reduction. A goal of five-weeks lead time in pre-manufacturing was set.

A multidisciplinary, multifunctional improvement team was created to spearhead the effort. Working under the improvement team were a number of subgroups that were assigned individual problems to study and asked to recommend corrections. Implementation was the joint responsibility of management and the process teams.

The improvement group looked at four areas, three of which were entirely internal to the company, and one of which involved suppliers in the first effort to create partnerships. The internal activities were:

- engineering;
- order entry;
- routing/rating

The fourth area was purchasing.

In this way, the company was able to take a redesign concept based on the president's radical ideas for reform and translate that blue-sky thinking into a small number of critical yet feasible projects.

Key Issues in Redesign

In the Redesign phase, a process improvement effort will focus on data collection, analysis, concept development, and specification of the various options. You will also seek to plan the realization phase and to obtain the consent of senior management to proceed (even if senior management is championing the effort from the start, it must at the end of this phase make a formal commitment to the implementation).

It is tempting in the analysis modules of work to conduct detailed analysis to the finest level of detail that can be achieved. This temptation must be resisted, although on occasion the team may go to the transaction level (e.g. phone call made, fax sent, etc.).

In practice much of the analysis will take place at higher levels than the transaction level and involve a series of activities (e.g. record order, etc.). A progressive refinement of the activities within each core business process is necessary to get to this level of analysis and requires a great deal of skill, as a continual and real-time balance must be made between the level of detail and the usefulness of the analysis for the effort.

It may be appropriate in some instances for a computer-based dynamic process simulator to be used in this analysis if there is an exceptional quantity of data.

PHASE 3   REALIZE—TIME TO IMPLEMENT

The tactics by which Business Process Reengineering is implemented have their roots in many different functional approaches to operational improvement.

- Information systems and control engineers have well-established approaches to project planning, monitoring, and control.
- Change management specialists, through their experiences of Total Quality and Time Based Management efforts in the 1980s, have well-defined training and group-based approaches for introducing incremental improvement.
- Finally, management experience gained largely through the need to consolidate different cultures rapidly in companies that have undergone mergers has shown how to create a new corporate style that helps the necessary changes to be introduced.

However, the power of Business Process Reengineering is in its scope as a company-wide effort. This scope requires that the work sets up a business-wide environment in which change can be successfully introduced. The improvement activities must allow for continual performance improvement, and project teams must undertake actions necessary to introduce the operational targets, new organizations, appraisal and reward systems, and processes that will achieve continued step changes in performance after the initial reengineering effort.

The Realize phase has five tracks, involving five different types of activities, as shown in Figure 4.4.

Together, these five tracks create a top-to-bottom transformation of the business's operations. The underlying principles of the Realize phase are well proven in organizational management: decisions must be based on facts, not intuition or hunches; the people who perform the work know it best; teams

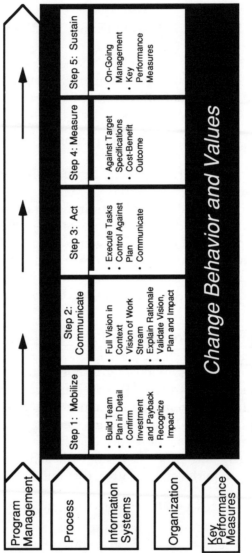

Figure 4.4 BreakPoint Framework: steps within phase 3.

can accomplish more than individuals alone and must be trained in structured problem-solving techniques.

Success in what is a complex effort will be best achieved if the business's needs for such action are clearly understood by all participants. The overall effort and milestones must be owned, understood by, and communicated clearly to all participants. This means that roles and responsibilities must be defined and communicated.

The handling of a complex company-wide effort such as this calls for skillful program management. Detailed consideration needs to be given in this phase to the establishment of work breakdown structures, as well as management and control procedures.

THE COUPLINGS COMPANY MOVES TOWARD A PROCESS ORIENTATION

Order Entry

In the old way of doing business, order entry went as follows:

1 The customer service group (reporting to sales) received the order via mail or, more often, telephone. The rep assigned the internal job order number and set up an order file.
2 The product management group (reporting to marketing) received the proposal from customer service, checked it against the order, and rewrote the customer service order, translating it into acceptable company nomenclature. They also set up a redundant order file.
3 The rewritten order was forwarded to credit for approval. Copies of credit acceptance were sent to customer service and product management; the order was forwarded to engineering.
4 In engineering, first a control clerk, then the working supervisor, reviewed the order, and assigned what was called a Phanjo (Phantom Job Order) number to the order before sending it to the Master Scheduler. The Phanjo was a placeholder, a "same-as except" order that indicated key work centers and anticipated capacity requirements. The Phanjo acted simply as a capacity reservation mechanism.
5 By determining backlog at the key centers the Master Scheduler could assign a due date and forward the order to customer

service for ship-date acknowledgement to the customer. A copy of the order was made and sent to engineering for design and detailing.

Although the process took eight days (64 hours), work sampling showed that only two hours of actual work was done to the order. (The order was being acted upon only 3 percent of the time it was in process, the rest of the time the order was in transit or waiting.) Flow charting showed that only 15 percent of actual operations performed on the order added value; 85 percent of the operations performed in the two hours the order was being acted on were wastes.

Looked at another way, of 98 operations performed, 32 were "move to"; 18 were "sort," "split," or "decide" where to move it; 15 were "do"; 18 were "review," "check," "change," or "correct"; and 15 were "copy," "recopy to new form," "file," or "pull file."

Only the 15 "do"s add value.

The largest queue (work-in-process inventory) was at the credit manager's desk. The explanation was that it required three to four days for a credit check by the outside agency. But there was never a credit hold on the 75 or so repeat customers.

Elimination of this bottleneck was simple: for regular customers a quarterly credit audit independent of an actual current order; for new customers a credit check in parallel with an assignment to engineering and the beginning of proposal development.

Another step was the creation of paperwork "cells" within product management. Since repeat customers tended to order the same type of thing, grouping orders by product type with specific customer service reps for product groups eliminated many hand-offs. These reps also took lead responsibility for proposal development and, since Phanjos were also oriented by product type, a little extra training allowed customer reps to assign Phanjos when they took the order, eliminating another bottleneck, at the engineering supervisor's desk.

Although the Master Scheduler's job remained intact, he was physically moved to an area accessible to all product management groups, creating a hub-and-spoke layout.

These changes allowed orders to get into the engineering queue in a fraction of the time. Intuitively, these solutions look simple. But just a few years earlier the company had undertaken a cost-cutting effort that had eliminated people from each department; however, because each department had been analyzed separately, that effort had done nothing to smooth or streamline the flow of work. Only when the process was analyzed as a whole was work made more efficient at the same time costs were cut.

Engineering

Under the old system, detail engineering required six weeks of throughput time. After the reengineering efforts, that was down to two weeks or less.

In addition to the imbalances caused by grouping by product size, about one-third of each group's time was taken away from all engineering by proposal preparation, which was given priority over designing for current projects. Work sampling in the engineering groups showed the following use of "productive" time:

Proposal preparation	32%
Design	18%
Detail	23%
Check	5%
Review order	5%
Reacquaint	11%
Reassignment	6%

Of the total time, 22 percent was spent either reacquainting an engineer with a job previously put down, transferring knowledge because of reassignment, or reviewing orders with the order entry group for clarification. The improvement group set goals to eliminate causes for interruptions.

A joint order entry/engineering group developed information checklists for each product type that allowed both groups to "do it right the first time" and eliminate interruptions from rechecking incomplete order entry information.

To reduce or eliminate reacquainting and reassigning, however, was more complex, necessitating either establishing a separate proposal group, reorganizing engineering along product-group lines, or a combination of both solutions. The improvement group recommended reorganizing along product-group lines with pro- posal writing in each group. But the steering committee rejected the proposal on the grounds that it made groups more specialized and "functional," rather than working on the engineering group's activities as processes, and working to a levelled demand.

Instead, a modified pull system was developed that manages the engineering queue and synchronizes it with the production plan in the shop. Under this system, whenever a job is completed in final assembly, a signal is sent to planning to release another job to the floor. The release of this job triggers a signal to the route/rate group to send one more job to production planning and to begin work on the next one in their queue, which in turn signals engineering.

Because of the variations in engineering time, the queue of completed jobs was allowed to float between four and two days. If it dipped below two days, engineers worked overtime; if it went above four days they were temporarily reassigned to improvement group work, tooling review, solving quality problems, and value-added analysis.

Under the old way, there was a need for a control clerk in each group to produce reports such as estimated time to completion and job cost tracking; but with lead time reduced to a number of days and a strict FIFO (first in, first out) pull system, there was no longer need for setting priorities and tracking jobs. Control clerks were reassigned or laid off. One bill of material clerk position was also eliminated after the shop went to manufacturing cells, reducing the bill of material detail and allowing the supervisor or operator to route from the blueprint.

In total, while reducing lead time from six weeks to less than two, staffing went from 27 to 16, a reduction of 41 percent. The success of the reengineering effort also showed that a computer-aided design (CAD) system could not be justified as either a time or labor-saving device because generic blueprints were employed, and engineering only dimensioned the drawings.

Routing/Rating

Once the product was designed, the routing/rating activity occurred. Routing is the activity that actually establishes the shopfloor machining and assembly sequence, while rating establishes standards for both cost accounting purposes and the purpose of establishing piecework rates. These activities usually had a three-week throughput time. Preliminary analysis showed it need not take nearly that long, and the improvement group set a goal of getting it below one week.

But before work on routing/rating activity could go forward, a number of other things had to happen.

First, since routing/rating was usually waiting on the arrival from a supplier of forging or steel round, there was never any hurry. Only after creating a process linkage with suppliers (discussed in the next section) could route/rate feel any pressure to reduce its throughput time.

In addition, although a few format changes to the Phanjo could reduce routing/rating throughput time immensely by providing route/rate with the complete basic routing information and allowing the manufacturing cell leader to do more of the detail routing, there was a more fundamental problem.

The standard hours reflected in the Phanjo were not acceptable to the piecework incentive system. The industrial engineer still required a routing to develop the appropriate rate. Thus, the issue came back to the basic incentive system the President had run up against at the beginning of his efforts to improve the company's performance.

Review of incoming job packets from engineering showed that the demand in routing/rating was highly irregular. At times the nine professionals in the department qualified to do the job were all needed, at other times most were working on their other activities, such as maintaining the work element file, performing check studies on disputed rates, developing new equipment justifications, programming numerically controlled machinery, and specifying tooling.

With the new pull system from the shop through engineering controlling the incoming flow to routing/rating of job packets, three of the nine professionals could be dedicated to the work. Balancing the other resources in the department meant that the entire time a job stayed in route/rate could be cut from 15 days to about $3\frac{1}{2}$ days.

Purchasing

Initial analysis showed that three commodities—steel rounds, forgings, and bearings—routinely took more time to order and receive than the one week the steering committee had set as a goal.

Under the old system, steel was purchased in large lot or mill quantities; forgings were purchased by whatever supplier had capacity at the time and could accommodate the due date.

Under the new system, a procurement strategy set the following objectives:

- Eliminate purchase orders, which take too much time and do not add value.
- Eliminate receiving inspection.
- Deliver to point of first use; first operation for steel and forgings, assembly for bearings.

- Only one vendor per commodity. The goal was to work closely with these vendors to connect the supply chain, creating mutual benefit for both the supplier and the company.
- Lead times in excess of seven days not tolerated; five or fewer days the norm.
- A 4 percent net cost reduction for each commodity.

Within these basic objectives, the strategies differed by commodity.

Steel

The improvement group felt the company could save time and money through reduced transportation and inventory by buying steel from a steel service center rather than directly from the mills. The service center manager showed the company extra savings; by having the service center saw the rounds to size (rather than the company buying bars and sawing as the first operation in gear manufacture), the company could eliminate two saws and one full-time operator. The service center could cut to size on more efficient equipment at a cost of two-thirds the direct labor of the operator alone.

In addition, by having the service center cut the bar to size, the company could eliminate the need for a sophisticated bar allocation system that was part of the computerized inventory control system. It took the equivalent time of one person to maintain that system. Eliminating the on-site cutting also eased the burden on route/rate personnel, and allowed the engineer to determine the length of the bar during design, making for a better product.

A simple truth was discovered in this effort; the vendor usually knows more about the intricacies of his product than the customer. By involving vendors at the earliest possible point, customers can often find considerable ways to improve the product, their processes, and their cost structure.

At the final analysis, the steel center was able to provide the company steel cut to length free on board (FOB) the new first operation (after eliminating sawing) with no transportation charge at a total cost of 6 percent less than the company was paying by buying steel and cutting it, and with a lead time of only three days.

Forgings

On initial analysis, reducing the lead time for the large (300–4000 pound) forgings would be a difficult task.

Forging suppliers argued that they needed backlog to assure sufficient billet stock (the company wanted five-day lead time and no backlog); they could not assure hammer availability since the forgings varied so widely in dimensions; and they did not want to tie up more than 15 percent of their capacity (roughly 60 percent of the company's requirements) with one single customer.

One potential supplier agreed to work with the improvement group on a more detailed analysis.

The first step in the more detailed analysis was to determine the factors the supplier considered when he assigned a forging to a hammer. For the company's forgings, the major factor was surface size or spread of metal. Once a means of quantification for analysis had been established it was relatively simple to identify the capacity requirements on each hammer. The analysis also showed there was relatively even demand for the two size ranges of forgings.

This allowed the procurement to be split among two suppliers— one of smaller-sized forgings, the other of larger-sized—and allayed the suppliers' fears of being held captive to a customer with more than 15 percent of their capacity.

The company addressed the forging suppliers' lead times, and found that, as in its own situation, order entry paperwork had a longer cycle than manufacturing (two weeks compared to three days). The purchasing improvement group found that when a proposal or bid was developed for one of its customers, a rough sketch of the forging was drawn by the design engineer and used to estimate raw material price and machining requirements. But that drawing was not transmitted to the forging supplier; rather, the supplier received a set of finished prints. So when an order went to the supplier, the forging drawings had to be redone by one of the supplier's draftsmen—a process that took almost all of the supplier's two-week order-entry lead time, including time in the queue.

By training the company's engineers in the forge shop's drawing requirements, the finished forging drawings could be completed in the proposal. With an agreement between the company and the sole-source forging supplier, a price formula was pre-negotiated. By transmitting the pre-priced proposal and drawings, the supplier's order-entry cycle was reduced to a few hours of editing and shop order generation. Over time, the supplier agreed that orders received by 11 a.m. would be at the forging company's first operation by 7 a.m. the next morning.

One of the two forging companies the company contracted with liked this system so much it instituted the same procedure with other large customers, eliminating two draftsmen and passing half the savings to the couplings company.

In its analysis of forgings, the company really did challenge all of its basic principles, to the point of getting engineers to change the way they did their work. The larger forgings were all made of the same alloy, but review of the smaller forgings found the frequent use of two major alloys and occasional use of three others.

It was determined that only one design engineer consistently specified the atypical alloys. When asked why, the engineer could only reply that no one had ever challenged him before, and that he felt that they were the most appropriate. Since no data could be found to support his gut feeling of the benefits of the particular alloy over more common ones, the engineer agreed to require the two alloys that were specified by the rest of the design group.

Bearings

Preliminary analysis of bearing demand showed irregular usage at the part number level, which forced the decision about whether to continue carrying bearings in stock or require a power transmission distributor to stock the bearings. Neither was acceptable.

Taking advantage of its parent company's position in the marketplace, the company surveyed power transmission distributors and found that although no distributor commonly stocked all of the bearings it needed, there was a reasonable national demand for all part numbers. The company was able to convince a national distributor to centralize its nationwide stock of the particular bearings it used in the local warehouse. This allowed the distributor to order at the maximum quantity break, be assured of reasonable inventory turns, and service both the company and its own financial objectives of high turn and increased growth—a win–win situation.

The assembly foreman now releases the required bearings two days prior to need, and the company pays an average of 4 percent less per bearing than it did before.

In the Final Analysis

The couplings company example shows the powerful results

that can be attained by keeping a few very basic principles in mind when conducting a reengineering effort:

1 Think of the entire core process, from the time the customer makes a connection with your company through the connections with suppliers and back to the customer.
2 Challenge everything that is done, constantly asking "why." The improvement group members more often than not received the typical answer: "because that's the way it's always been done."
3 Process improvement efforts cannot be allowed to push problems upstream on to suppliers; the goal should be creating "virtuality" in the process by including the supplier and its expertise in an effort to streamline and upgrade the entire process. Relations with suppliers need to be "win–win."
4 Take the process improvement to the marketplace; use the business process reengineering effort to capture and control markets, or to seek out new markets.

In four months of process improvement efforts the company was able to reduce the overall lead time from between 28 and 32 weeks to between 10 and 11 weeks (without even working on the part of the process inside the manufacturing operation). Headcount reduction was 29 percent, from 56 to 40 people. Inventory reduction potential approached $8 million. Purchased price net reduction in materials was $530 000 (roughly twice the previous year's achievement) for the first year.

Most important, sales volume remained steady despite a 20 percent decrease in the size of the overall market. One of the three competitors ceased manufacturing of engineered products, and the company almost doubled its overall market share, picking up the majority of the failed company's market share.

Keeping the doors open

goal — new products
look at Gordup

Outline —
fill in

Committee to make ✓ off
design focus groups
12

5
Searching for BreakPoints

The design-for-excellence project at AT&T's Dallas power systems facility was not the first time Andy Guarriello had conducted a successful Business Process Reengineering effort. In 1987, in Shreveport, LA, AT&T had reengineered the process for producing the 10-button Merlin telephone and achieved stunning—BreakPoint—results.

The goal at the beginning of that undertaking had been survival, it was simply not justifiable to manufacture the business phone in the United States when it could be made so much less expensively in Singapore. As shown in Figure 5.1, a Just-In-Time effort reduced the cost of goods sold; further reduction was achieved through a redesign of the telephone, including the embedding of the external speaker in the telephone itself in speakerphone models. This was a technological breakthrough accomplished as part of the vision of a potential BreakPoint. This concept of creating a vision of a BreakPoint that necessitates a technological breakthrough will be discussed in greater detail later in this chapter.

Finally, through further reengineering, the total cost of goods sold (COGS) was reduced by about three-fourths, making the phone less expensive to build in the United States than if it were built in Singapore and shipped to the United States. This allowed AT&T not only to solidify its hold on much of the U.S. market, but actually to capture market share in the

Shreveport 10 Button Merlin

Relative Cost of Goods

	Original	JIT Pilot	Redesign	JIT/DFM
Material	100	95	87	62
Labor/Load	100	74	67	51
Speaker	100	100	0(Incl.)	0(Incl.)
Total Cost/Unit	100	94	36	26

Figure 5.1 A Just-In-Time effort to reduce costs.

Far East. In addition, the company stockpiled a BreakPoint in case any competitor began to catch up in North America.

As seen in Figure 5.1, the Just-In-Time effort reduced the cost of materials by 5 percent and labor by 26 percent—reason enough to cheer and justify the effort. But enhancement within the factory's four walls was not enough for Shreveport; the plant was on a mission to develop a product and process that would be a BreakPoint and create a disproportionate reaction in the marketplace.

AT&T's Bell Laboratories in New Jersey were given the task of reducing material and labor cost further, and redesigning the product. They came back with the innovative technology that embedded the speaker in the phone and reduced other costs. Again, in and of itself, this is reason to cheer the effort.

But the design was accomplished in an "operations vacuum," and although the product was a cost success there were obvious design improvements that would make the product more compatible with the manufacturing process.

Bell Laboratories and the factory worked together to develop manufacturing, test and design rules that would harmonize the improvements with the operations process. Basically, the company redesigned the "design for production" process, and in doing so realized an astounding 74 percent reduction in cost.

This is a classic story of finding a value-chain-oriented Break-Point, this one in the realm of cost. It shows clearly how the development of a winning value-chain strategy is:

- based on process effectiveness;
- clearly defined;
- linked to a vision of the marketplace.

Successful value-chain strategies are *daringly pragmatic*, with a focus on core business processes; and because of the definition of core business processes, operations always has a central role in the strategy. Defining and pursuing BreakPoints adds a new dimension to the old way of defining strategy. Looking at potential BreakPoints helps you define tasks, activities, and finally processes, that can lead to the accomplishment of the strategic goal. In effect, the search for BreakPoints redefines the marketplace strategy by identifying not only the who, what and where, but the *how*.

WHAT EXACTLY IS A BREAKPOINT?

Although the concept of BreakPoint has been touched on before, a clear definition is necessary. A *BreakPoint* is the achievement of excellence in one or more value metrics where the marketplace clearly recognizes the advantage, and where the ensuing result is a disproportionate and sustained increase in the supplier's market share.

Figure 5.2 shows the five areas of operations where Break-Points can occur—market, product design and support, value chain, and finance, as well the information systems umbrella —and the value metrics in each operational area. This book, as has been said, is focusing on the value metrics in the value chain, as well as the area of design and service in the product area and information systems. Information systems can also be a BreakPoint, if they speed or simplify the external connections within the core business process.

Let us look briefly at the eight value-chain BreakPoint elements, as well as three related elements from the product

MARKET	PRODUCT	VALUE CHAIN	FINANCE
Reaching New Customers	Time to Develop New Product	Price of Product	Cost of Funds
Promoting Product		Robustness of Product	Source of Funds
Time to Market	Design of Product	Lead time Manufacture	Product Financing
Responsiveness to Change	Technology of Product	Flexibility of Production	Financial Stability
	Support for the Product	Process Design	
Pricing of Product		Delivery Reliability	
Certification of Product	- Field Service	Product Differentiation/	
	- Technical Service	Optionality	
	- Service Empathy	Environmental Proaction	

Information

Figure 5.2 *BreakPoint value metrics—examples.*

area. To achieve a BreakPoint, it is imperative to manage the core business processes, in both their operational aspects and the way they connect with the customer or the supplier external to the company's internal operations.

The market defines what it wants in the following terms:

- robustness;
- price;
- lead time;
- flexibility;
- process design;
- reliability;
- differentiation/optionality;
- environmental proaction;
- product design;
- service empathy;
- information systems.

Each of these market desires, in turn, can be measured in terms of the four value metrics: quality, cost, time, and service, each in a different proportion. For instance, price seems like cost, but a customer might be willing to pay a higher price for better quality, faster delivery, or better after-sales service, although cost is still the largest component of price.

Robustness

This element pertains to all physical attributes of a product, and has been well documented by such companies as Toyota. A product's robustness refers to its fitness for use, ease of manufacture, and even its ability to be recycled; for example, the Bavarian Motor Works (BMW) worked hard to develop a car that is totally recyclable, and achieved a BreakPoint in environmentally conscious areas of Europe, although not in the United States (possibly because this effort coincided with a recession and a trend toward "buying American" in the United States in the late 1980s and early 1990s). In another effort, by tying "the voice of the customer," with rigorous process capability improvement, Ford achieved a BreakPoint when it introduced the Taurus/Sable models.

Price

The 74 percent cost reduction achieved by AT&T discussed above allowed the company to drop its price in the Far East to undercut the competition in order to establish a new market position.

Lead Time

By reducing the replenishment lead time, the spare parts division of a major automotive manufacturer improved service-ability from a 93 percent fill rate to 98 percent and now enjoys the top service rating among its competitors. Coincidently, by reducing the lead time, it was able successfully to close 8 of its 18 parts-distribution centers and reduced inventory by $1 billion.

Lead time was also the BreakPoint for Motorola in the pager business. It knew it not only would have to meet competitive quality and price targets to compete with the Japanese, but early on set a goal to surpass the Japanese competition by being able to receive an order, manufacture the pager, and uniquely configure the pager, all within a few hours. The Japanese could not compete in the U.S. market, given the freight lead times imposed by the distance from the point of manufacture to the customer's location.

Flexibility

Flexibility is defined as an ability to respond immediately to a customer requirement. Ideally, by synchronizing capacity with customer usage, there is total flexibility to respond to mix variance. But true flexibility goes beyond that definition.

For instance, in the highly competitive and fad conscious snack food industry, new product introductions traditionally require new process equipment even though the basic technology for manufacture is similar to that of current products.

Because one company took 4 to 6 hours to change over a continuous oven, it had a policy of buying a new, expensive oven every time it test marketed a new product. Introduction of new products (sometimes even test marketing) became a board of directors issue, since the board had to approve a capital appropriation. By implementing Predictive Control methodologies, the changeover has been reduced to 15 minutes, with a goal of 5 minutes. Flexibility has given the company the opportunity to test market many products that may previously have never seen the market. The company's overall share grew 11 percent in just two years.

Process Design

Hewlett-Packard made a simple videotape of a game that explained the principle of Just-In-Time. Allen-Bradley developed a fully automated assembly line that featured its cell controllers. Motorola, Xerox, and others have won the U.S. Commerce Department's Malcolm Baldrige Award for quality. AT&T won the Shingo Award. By improving their manufacturing process to a level of leadership, these companies' enhanced images in the market have resulted in BreakPoints.

Reliability

For purposes of this discussion, reliability does not have a strong quality connotation; but rather more one of reliable delivery of sequenced components to the point of use a few minutes before installation (such as automobile seats and brake systems). A company that can achieve this level of reliability can force its customer to use it as a single source of components.

Differentiation/Optionality

A diesel engine manufacturer differentiates itself by having the capability of machining straight, tight tolerance holes with consistent surface finish. This ability took years of variation research and continuous improvement to perfect.

A manufacturer of sweaters developed a mechanism to handle the yarn in such a manner that the nap is raised when the garment is knitted. The result is a garment that is both pleasing to the eye and lasts longer.

A maker of power transformers offered dozens of different KVA options. By rationalizing the number of options the company was able to upgrade the KVA specification (providing greater safety) and offer the transformer at the lower KVA price.

Environmental Proaction

Monsanto Co.'s chemicals group has created a benevolent market image by stressing its care for the environment through strict plant, material, and process controls. And by lobbying for higher standards, Monsanto has become the *de facto* manager of regulations. While the company is playing the role of "green knight," its competitors are finding that it is two to three times more expensive to retrofit to meet the new standards (in effect imposed by Monsanto) in addition to dealing with payments into the U.S. Superfund to clean up pollution that are on average 10 times more costly than designing a process that prevents pollution.

Product Design

In the past, the design function operated relatively independently of the manufacturing process. But with the advent of quality process capability loops, design for manufacture/ assembly software, group technology techniques, and early manufacturing involvement (EMI) teams, design engineering has become an enabler to value-chain excellence.

The AT&T business telephone example describes the synergistic BreakPoint achieved.

Service Empathy

The President & CEO of Security Insurance articulated in 1987 as part of his vision for the company "customer service as a mission," through "dedicated and committed people" and a "highly efficient organization." Through research begun in 1983 the company had determined that there are only a few vital criteria that affect service quality perception: reliability, responsiveness, assurance, empathy, and certain apparent tangibles such as physical facilities.

Empathy, defined as caring, individualized attention to customers, is all important. Security Insurance's customer service strategy said, in part, "we will make every effort to understand our customers' needs and provide individualized attention." This is done through a quality staff that has the "knowledge, confidence and attitude to provide the right answer every time." Staff need to be "accessible and available to meet our customers' needs and expectations, especially in emergencies."

The company developed a credo: "Fast, Accurate & Caring— Every Time," and was rewarded with increased market share.

Information Systems

While the other attributes are potential BreakPoints that fall within the group of product or value chain, information

systems cut across all boundaries. In any effort to effe
a BreakPoint, information systems must be utilized to
their fullest. In some instances, the BreakPoint cannot be
totally achieved without breakthrough use of information
systems.

Beyond the obvious benefits of management information
systems, there has been the maturation of electronic point of
sale pull signals and expert systems. For products requiring
configuration control, key customers' design engineering
groups can be given access to the supplier's engineering data
base so that they may design the appropriate options, thus
avoiding the numerous iterations between customer and
supplier. Not only does this approach lock in the supplier,
but it significantly reduces the customer's design-to-market
time.

Lithonia Lighting carried the expert system approach one
step further. Its dealers/agents and architectural specifiers can
directly order or design from the host computer. The factory's
flexible manufacturing systems can be swiftly modified for new
product groups that the market demands.

BREAKPOINT PROCESS REDESIGN CHARACTERISTICS

Core business processes in which there may be a BreakPoint
have a number of key characteristics:

1 They require the most radical type of process redesigns,
because of the large difference between the actual and
theoretical capabilities of the process.
2 The advantage to the customer and/or supplier clearly exists
and results in an improved relationship.
3 They are responsive to external competitive or regulatory
pressures.
4 They could become the key source of competitiveness and
the key means of sustaining the advantage, and the key to
management of the market.

After implementing the BreakPoint approach to reengineering, successfully reengineered processes have these characteristics:

1 They drive business strategy by defining the what, where, and, most importantly, how.
2 They represent—or sometimes define—core business capabilities.
3 They can be envisioned as successive BreakPoints and stockpiled.
4 They have become the key source of competitiveness and the key means of sustaining the advantage, and the key to the management of the market.

Most businesses view gain in market share as incremental, and as moving in straight-line slopes. But BreakPoints in and of themselves lead to a reaction by competitors to try to mitigate the disproportionate market-share gain. So BreakPoints should be positioned similarly to the classic successive technology "S" curves, and the concept must include a series of BreakPoints to be stockpiled and introduced to the market when required, rather than just one BreakPoint, as seen in Figure 5.3.

Example: Semi-Conductor
What Could Result From Process Re-engineering:

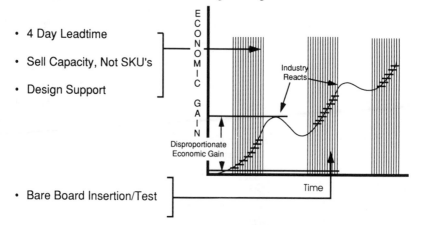

Figure 5.3 *Stockpiling of BreakPoints.*

For instance, for the semiconductor company that discovered the BreakPoint of four-day delivery anywhere, it stockpiled the BreakPoint of partially populating boards for customers. The benefit of this to the company would be the opportunity to sell more devices on one board and simplify the test procedure by performing some tests *in situ* rather than individually. The customer would have to do less work, and would enjoy lower overall acquisition costs, lower inventories, and faster throughput times.

LISTEN TO THE CUSTOMER (MARKET), BUT HEAR THE PROCESS

Listening to the Customer

In Chapter 4, we discussed the ideas of determining core business processes, processes that support core processes, and non-core processes, then deciding which process to work on improving, mapping all steps in the process, and then finding out which activities can be eliminated or streamlined in order to get a reengineered process.

When searching for BreakPoints, one needs to stop here for a moment and, instead of going straight on into an effort to make the processes more efficient and effective, do a little market research, to listen to the voice of the customer.

Over a short period, in either one-on-one face-to-face interviews or small focus groups, customers and/or potential customers are assembled. The first half of the survey is blind: questions are asked without revealing the name of the company that is asking. Questions are asked about the customer's requirements for the supplied commodity and about the market parity requirements, what a company needs to be doing today to be competitive. The second half of the survey asks specifically about the company doing the asking, in order to determine the surveying company's perceived strengths and weaknesses, and the "get right" requirements for the industry—what the marketplace would like to see companies do in the future.

Some people feel they do not have to do this, that their understanding of the market they sell into is quite good. Regardless of how long a company has been selling in a particular market, or how good it believes its current market intelligence to be, this is an important exercise to carry out in a formal way as part of the effort to identify BreakPoints.

For example, the marketplace told the semiconductor company first described in Chapter 1 that the near-term get-rights on a somewhat macro level were:

- reliable delivery +/– one day;
- two-week lead time;
- order status inquiry;
- negotiable special terms and prices;
- flexibility for volume changes.

If the market research had been done in a more rigorous manner, it would have been possible to quantify the customer's current and future expectations; or what the marketplace wants in terms of:

- price (cost);
- quality (ppm);
- service (delivery +/– period);
- time (both design time-to-market and replenishment lead time);
- optionality (more/less);
- flexibility (+/– % capacity swing; +/– % mix swing).

Such customer interviews also help a company to understand better the market forces acting on an industry—the "drivers" discussed in Chapter 2. In addition, the interviews should help companies determine what their current core business processes are by the emphasis customers put on various aspects of operations in the industry. For example, if a number of customers say that they would like to see faster release of new products by any supplier, it is pretty easy to see that new product development is a core business process; if customers say they would like to see shorter lead times, order entry may be defined as a core business process, although in the past it had been seen as a supporting process.

With this information, a company can begin to determine the "get rights," what must be done to stay competitive; as well as the potential BreakPoints, and the competitive thrusts a company could take if it wants to try to change the direction of an industry by finding BreakPoints that redefine core business processes.

Figure 5.4 shows the area a company might focus on when

Product Design to Market

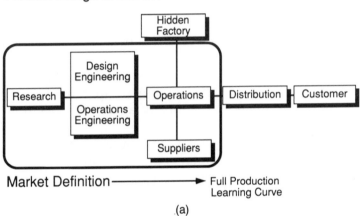

(a)

Or, Quick Response

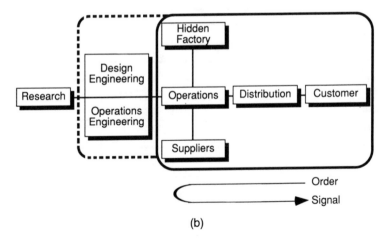

(b)

Figure 5.4 *Process boundaries.*

looking for a potential BreakPoint when the market says faster new product development is a highly desired aspect of business (Figure 5.4(a)), and the area the company might focus on if quick response (flexibility) is shown by the market research to be in demand (Figure 5.4(b)).

Boundaries are drawn around the activities that make up the process that could provide a BreakPoint. In all of this work on creating a vision, the participants should think "blue sky,"— "wouldn't it be great if we could ..."

At the same time, what we call a "best practice vs. can do" map is created, taking all of the BreakPoint variables of robustness, price, etc., and comparing the company's offerings against those of competitors. A hypothetical example is shown in Figure 5.5.

Another way to think of this is to ask the questions: "What are we good at?" and "What are our competitors better at?" The areas for comparing a company against competition are shown in Figure 5.6.

This is really the beginning of "visioning," where the group challenges the basic assumptions of the existing process. For example, response time in the banking industry clearly translates into dollars—the faster a bank can process cash the greater

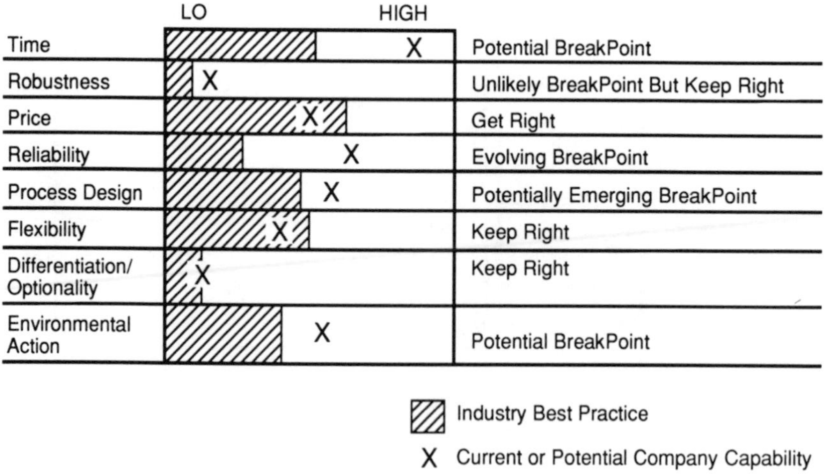

	LO	HIGH	
Time		X	Potential BreakPoint
Robustness	X		Unlikely BreakPoint But Keep Right
Price	X		Get Right
Reliability		X	Evolving BreakPoint
Process Design		X	Potentially Emerging BreakPoint
Flexibility	X		Keep Right
Differentiation/ Optionality	X		Keep Right
Environmental Action		X	Potential BreakPoint

▨ Industry Best Practice

X Current or Potential Company Capability

Figure 5.5 *"Best practice vs. can do" map.*

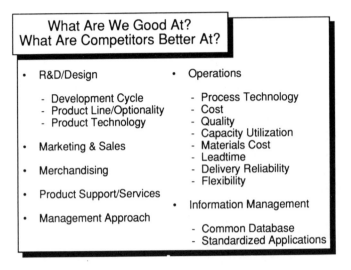

What Are We Good At?
What Are Competitors Better At?

- R&D/Design

    - Development Cycle
    - Product Line/Optionality
    - Product Technology

- Marketing & Sales

- Merchandising

- Product Support/Services

- Management Approach

- Operations

    - Process Technology
    - Cost
    - Quality
    - Capacity Utilization
    - Materials Cost
    - Leadtime
    - Delivery Reliability
    - Flexibility

- Information Management

    - Common Database
    - Standardized Applications

Figure 5.6 Comparing a company against competition.

the opportunity to manage the ensuing cash float to its advantage, and the happier the customer is with the bank's responsiveness.

One particular bank going through the visioning process determined that mail took four–six hours to be sorted and distributed to the appropriate processing group. The team looked for ways to speed up the mailroom process. What they should have done, however, was ask "why do we have the mailroom?" When the entire process is mapped, it is easy to see that the Post Office has to sort the mail. Currently, the Post Office combines all the bank's mail and delivers it to the bank's mailroom, where it is resorted for the processing centers. Why not have different box numbers at the Post Office and have each box's contents delivered directly to the correct processing center?

Another example involves an operation in the manufacture of plastic sunglasses. After the temple and frames were molded they were passed over a small, open flame to remove the flash left by the molding process. By challenging the activity as not adding value, the team determined that the flame treating activity was necessary because of poor maintenance of the mold, and if the mold's mating surfaces were kept in a truly flat geometry there would be no flash and no need for flame treating.

The company team that encountered this problem went through the following exercise of challenging the assumptions, practices, and value-adding steps.

First, they challenged the value added by each step.

Molding the frame and temple clearly adds value; transporting to quality control does not; inspecting does not; sorting the right and left bows and stacking does not; flame treating does not. At this point there was a disagreement about whether flame treating added value; some people said the product was physically changed (one of the tests under the Just-In-Time definition of adding value). So the group questioned closely why flame treating was necessary.

Q. Why is it necessary to flame treat?
A. Because there is a plastic parting line that would cause discomfort for the wearer.
Q. Why is there a parting line?
A. Because the mold faces don't meet.
Q. Why don't they meet?
A. Because they aren't maintained flat.
Q. Why aren't they maintained?
A. Because no one ever questioned it before, we just corrected by heat treating.

On the group went: transporting to stock does not add value; storing does not; transporting to assembly does not; transfer printing does (transfer printing refers to printing a designer's name on the eyeglass temple, a marketing step that allows the glasses to command a premium price—far more than the cost of the activity—and hence adds value); transporting to hinging does not; and so on.

In conclusion, only two of the ten steps add value, *and it took 10 weeks to go from step one to step ten,* and this was a seasonal business.

Hearing the Process

After listening to the customer's understanding of the marketplace, and description of what constitutes competitive parity and what will need to be done in the future to maintain a competitive position, one goes back to the process and creates a value metric map. For each activity, cost is mapped, using activity-based costing standards; quality, using first-pass yield; time, using queue hours; and service, as measured by throughput time variance.

A value metric map might look like Figure 5.7.

The spikes on the map represent opportunities. The highest spikes when benchmarked against competitors indicate either an industry "get right" or competitive advantage. The higher the spike, the larger the problem. However, this is also the place where the larger opportunities for BreakPoints occur. Each spike needs to be challenged for value added, purpose, assumptions, and principles as described later in this chapter. After exhaustive challenging and brainstorming, a picture or vision of the "can be" emerges. Then it remains to check whether that can-be vision is indeed a BreakPoint by reading the market again.

CREATING THE VISION

At this point, key management personnel need to meet to take this information gathered from listening to the marketplace and hearing the process, and from that create a vision for where the company could go that would give it a surge into marketplace dominance. What they are looking for is disconnects, what they can deliver that the marketplace has not yet identified as important and, in fact, has no concept is possible.

This vision of what the company might be able to do is measured against what the company does well and what the current industry best practice is in order to analyze gaps.

After the process has been mapped and it has been determined what the company does better than its competitors and vice versa; once the challenging has been done and the core processes have been bounded; once these gaps have been analyzed, then the company goes back and rereads the market-

128

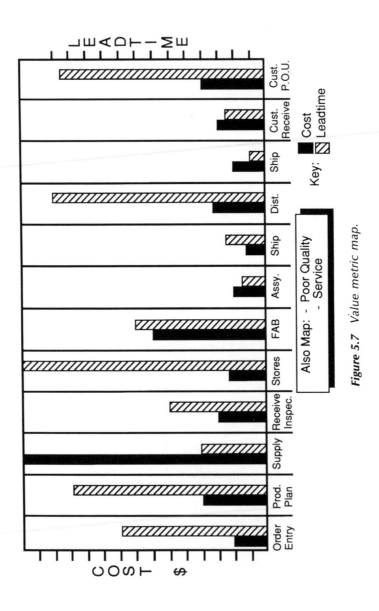

Figure 5.7 *Value metric map.*

place to see what the marketplace would consider a real Break-
Point (i.e. does the market want what the company believes it
can provide? Will what the company can deliver create a
disproportionate reaction in the market?). This second round of
market research must be done in this way because the marketplace does not know what the company knows about what
its process is capable of; therefore, in effect, the marketplace
does not know what it is possible to ask for and successfully
receive.

This is done using a carefully constructed designed experiment, in which marketplace participants are asked what
combination of attributes they would most like to see the
company provide.

A full factorial designed experiment would be very expensive, since as the number of potential BreakPoints increased the
number of experiments would need to grow factorially. But
statistical research has shown that if a company has, for
instance, seven potential BreakPoints, it can lay out an array of
eight cards, each with a possible combination of attributes, as
shown in Figure 5.8. Each of at least 32 potential buying

Orthogonal Array Table

Col.	1 A	2 B	3 C	4 D	5 E	6 F	7 G	Ranking
Exp. # 1	P	P	P	P	P	P	P	X
2	P	P	P	C	C	C	C	
3	P	C	C	P	P	C	C	
4	P	C	C	C	C	P	P	
5	C	P	C	P	C	P	C	
6	C	P	C	C	P	C	P	
7	C	C	P	P	C	C	P	
8	C	C	P	C	P	P	C	N

Key:
P = Market Parity
C = Can Do

Figure 5.8 *Taguchi experimental design.*

influences is then asked to rank the cards in order of the combination of attributes they would most like. This ranking by a limited number of parties can be used to predict statistically whether any factor has a major impact on the marketplace, or whether that factor is merely "noise".

Designed experiments have been used for many years in the area of quality. In a brainstorming session, a group creates a fishbone diagram of possible causes for a problem, then creates a designed experiment in which the causes are not randomly varied, but controlled. By running the operation under these varying sets of conditions, it can be determined which causes are real and which are artificial.

In the same way, when preparing a market read of potential BreakPoints, each is assigned two values—one is market parity, the other "can do." For example, if lead time were tested on the electronics customers of the semiconductor company, the lead time market parity value would be two weeks and the "can do" value would be four days.

Each of the cards has the factors (or values if you want to describe the options that way) alternated according to the controlled array. The market respondents are then asked to arrange the cards in order of a most to least preferred sequence. Assigning numerical values to each position in the high–low sequence, a statistical analysis can be performed on the responses and the BreakPoints can be identified and quantified.

The next task is for the company to determine which Break-Points it wants to go after. This is done by first working out a high-level implementation plan, which in turn determines the degree of difficulty in achieving the can do or BreakPoint values. The degree of difficulty and the degree of market reaction as determined by the designed experiment are plotted as shown in Figure 5.9.

As the final step before actually implementing the reengineering efforts that will lead to the BreakPoint, the company must specifically define the mission and objectives of each process that will be reengineered. Figure 5.10 shows the mission and objectives of the semiconductor company's Break-Point core business processes.

More than likely the company will choose to go after the "gimmes" first and save the "stretch" BreakPoints in a

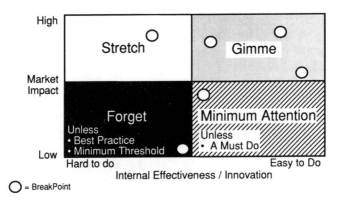

Figure 5.9 *BreakPoint prioritization map.*

stockpile, assuming that while the company is enjoying the fruits of the first BreakPoint, it is working hard to achieve one or more others for the stockpile, and that the methodological lessons learned from achieving the first BreakPoint make it easier to go after subsequent BreakPoints.

There is a final difference between reengineering core processes for parity or achieving best in class and going after BreakPoints. The standard reengineering effort can be sustained for some time using continuous improvement tools

---

Define Specific Mission/Objectives of Order Realization Process

For Example:

Mission:
> Provide a System to Manufacture and Ship Quality Product Within 4 Days of Order Receipt From the Key 39 Customers and Receive Payment 3 Days Later.

Objectives:
- Cost Reduction of 24%
- Maintain Same High Quality Levels
- Space Reduction of 45%
- Capacity Increase of 40%
- Accurately Reflect Real Product Cost

Figure 5.10 *Mission and objectives of semiconductor company's BreakPoint processes.*

and techniques, but BreakPoint reengineering demands the constant search for new BreakPoints. There is no steady continuous improvement, only leaps and bounds in market-place dominance.

A BREAKPOINT IN CONTROLLING THE SUPPLY CHAIN: THE ORDER-FULFILLMENT PROCESS

Part I   The Carpet Industry

The traditional supply chain for carpeting is as follows.

A fiber manufacturer makes the carpet fiber, then trucks it to another plant where the yarn is spun. The yarn is then sold to a carpet mill, where the yarn is woven into a backing material, then dyed. This dyeing operation is undertaken according to a forecast: so many yards of weave X need to be dyed dark blue each month to provide for warehouse needs and those of retailers.

Another section of the carpet mill applies a sturdy backing and shears the rolls to a uniform size. The finished rolls are stored offsite in a carpet mill warehouse awaiting retail orders.

The retailer orders the rolls, usually to his own forecast or on the basis of some promotional incentive from the mill, then puts the rolls into his stock. Once a customer sale is made the retailer cuts the roll to size and installs it at the customer's site.

Average cumulative lead time for the entire process is 16 weeks. The cost, based on a fiber cost of $1.00/lb for our manufacturer, a major American fiber producer, is $5.34/square yard to the retailer, as shown in Figure 5.11.

The economic forces of 1989–90 were such that many carpet retailers were going out of business. Remaining retailers were forced to compete heavily on price in order to stay in business. Some carpet mills were entering the retail market with their own distribution outlets, in effect competing against their own customers.

To fight back, some large retailers were developing house brands, which further eroded carpet mill margins and in turn forced price pressures upon the upstream yarn manufacturers. Some fiber manufacturers were fighting the mills by consumer branding their products so they could extract a premium (e.g. Monsanto's "Weardated.") Even so, income before taxes (IBT) had shrunk by 84 percent industrywide.

Not unexpectedly, the entire industry was suffering from over capacity in a market that remained flat.

As Is: Large Throughput/Cycle Times, Massive Inventory

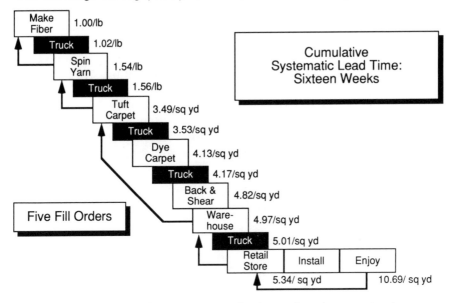

Figure 5.11 *Cumulative systematic lead time for carpet production.*

Carpet mills were beginning either to integrate backwards by absorbing yarn houses, or to investigate starting up yarn-making facilities. One mill actually studied the options and determined that the outsourcing versus vertical integration was a 2.5 percent cost advantage to themselves. They tentatively shelved the idea of verticle integration for a number of reasons:

1 Large organizations tend to be unwieldy (most carpet mills are relatively small organizations that focus not on technology, but on consumer marketing).
2 Yarn technology requires significant R&D investment.
3 The enormous amount of capital required to start up a fiber/yarn facility was not readily available in 1989–90 due to the market conditions.

At the same time, retailers and consumers were increasingly demanding responsiveness. Ideally, the retailers wanted "immediate" delivery of cut-piece orders. Once the consumer commits to a style and color, he or she wants delivery and installation "now". Studies had shown that both the retailer and the consumer are generally willing to pay a small premium for such responsiveness.

Not only did the retailer/consumer group want immediate response, but they wanted variety. A study by the fiber manufacturer involved in this effort and its key customers indicated that there was significant proliferation of stock keeping units (SKUs) at each level of manufacture: 40 different yarns, 134 different greiges (undyed carpet stage), and an overwhelming 2909 choices at the dyed carpet level.

The double forces of responsiveness and variety, coupled with price pressures, argued for a new way of thinking for the carpet industry. Right from the start of its efforts to reengineer the order-fulfillment process, this particular manufacturer knew that continuous improvement was not going to be the mechanism to survive, much less to dominate.

Part II The Company

In the early 1980s, the fiber manufacturer had the dominant branded fiber and enjoyed significant market growth. It was the industry leader in new-product development, product performance was excellent, and the company was highly profitable.

For these reasons, customer relations were excellent. The company was a critical part in the success of its parent company, which was then purely in the chemicals business. Through a series of acquisitions in a number of unrelated industries during the decade, the parent company became a conglomerate and grew four-fold. While much of senior management's attention was taken up learning the new businesses and integrating all of the acquisitions, the fiber manufacturing company was allowed to fall from its position of dominance.

By 1990, the fiber company was a shell of its former self. It had the third ranked branded fiber, the lowest compound annual growth (CAG) in the industry, had become a high-cost producer, and was consequently losing market share.

By its own admission, the company had no strategic focus. Operationally, it continued to schedule to forecast, had below average process control technology, produced in large lot sizes because of slow changeovers, and focused almost entirely on labor cost reduction in a relatively non-labor-intensive industry (an outlook imposed by strict hurdle rates—one to two years payback—necessitated by the corporate need to fund expansion into other industries).

The company's accounting system was arcane. Critical reports required manual calculation and/or reconciliation. Monthly closings sometimes stretched out beyond the next month's actual close. Product costs were inappropriate because of multiple and often inaccurate allocations upon variable factory labor (which represented only 2–3 percent of the total cost of goods). Lacking financial accuracy, the "focused" cost-reduction projects were in reality unfocused since the accounting system obscured knowledge of where the real cost opportunities resided.

Finally, lead times for fiber manufacture and spinning were as much as nine weeks.

In short, the fiber company was in no way positioned for meeting the increasing consumer/retailer demand of variety and responsiveness.

Part III   Breaking the China and Determining the BreakPoint

Management of the fiber company finally realized that the company was behind the pack and slipping fast. Excuses were aired, and hands were wrung. They were introduced to the concept of radical change as represented by BreakPoints and, although many were inclined to take the bull by the horns and make a dramatic effort to recapture and dominate the market, they simply did not know where to begin. But they understood where the company was, realized what the market wanted and, most importantly, realized that the company had to set a new, dramatic course if it was to regain and eventually surpass its past prominence in the industry.

The company recognized that in order to provide responsiveness to customers, it needed to regain control of the value chain—what is called the Demand Driving Point—that had been relinquished, first to the carpet mills and then to the retailer. The management correctly realized that for responsiveness to become a BreakPoint, inventory would need to be located at the point of the fewest stock units—SKUs (the company had 40 while the retailer had 2909).

Management was intuitively coming to the key lesson in what is called Demand Driven Logistics. While in Quick Response the retailer is, by default, the Demand Driving Point, in Demand Driven Logistics one or more upstream players usually becomes the Demand Driving Point. If the manufacturer sets itself up as the Demand Driving Point, moving itself closer to the end user by collapsing intermediate steps, it both creates a situation where it can actively manage the market and at the same time puts itself in a position to be most responsive to market demand changes.

Successful Demand Driven Logistics creates advantages for every participant along the supply chain, especially the manufacturer who is successful setting itself up as the Demand Driving Point, by almost locking in customers (retailers) because of the advantage.

To see how, let us look at the rest of the fiber company's "daringly pragmatic" vision.

Figure 5.12 shows this vision, with the retailer, carpet mill and fiber manufacturer linked so tightly in production that they are *virtually one entity*.

In this vision, when a customer orders a carpet from a retailer, the retailer in turn places an order on the fiber manufacturer and reserves capacity at the mill (the dictum of Demand Driven Logistics, "buy capacity, not SKUs"). The customer order figuratively pulls the requirement through the value chain. The specific carpet size and color is made and installed in one week.

The company realized this vision would be dependent on three things:

1   The total actual production and transport time would have to be five days. The key to making this work would be minimal lot sizes and cycle times (cycle time = value added throughput time plus

Should Be:

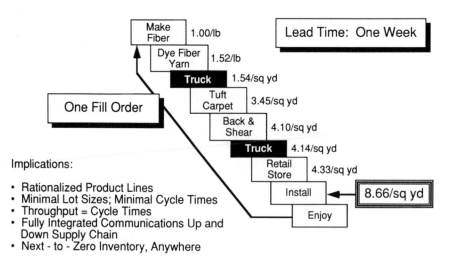

Make Fiber 1.00/lb
Dye Fiber Yarn 1.52/lb
Truck 1.54/sq yd
Tuft Carpet 3.45/sq yd
Back & Shear 4.10/sq yd
Truck 4.14/sq yd
Retail Store 4.33/sq yd
Install 8.66/sq yd
Enjoy

Lead Time: One Week

One Fill Order

Implications:

• Rationalized Product Lines
• Minimal Lot Sizes; Minimal Cycle Times
• Throughput = Cycle Times
• Fully Integrated Communications Up and Down Supply Chain
• Next - to - Zero Inventory, Anywhere

Figure 5.12   Fiber company's pragmatic vision.

transport, if necessary), and fully integrated communications up and down the supply chain.

2   In order to reduce the total production and transport time to three days, a technical breakthrough would need to be made. (This is often the case, the discussion of "wouldn't it be great if we could ..." leads to the comment "but that will need new technology." The implicit understanding that the current technology is *the* technology often keeps people from thinking in a daringly pragmatic way.)

In this case, the technological breakthrough would be a way to dye fiber uniformly *before* it was woven as a rug rather than dyeing the rug. The traditional dyeing process is not complex, merely time consuming. A roll of carpet is literally hand fed—by very strong men—into a large vat. The drying process, even when speeded up by heating, can take as much as 24 hours. Taking one of the five total cycle time days just to dry the carpet was out of the question.

Dyeing fiber or yarn had long been a twinkle in the eye of the R&D chemists. Now the business imperative would force them to take the task seriously and create Solution Dyed Nylon.

3   The final part of turning the vision into a reality would be the creation of Strategic Alliance Mills (SAMs). The fiber company would find "a few good customers" who would form the nucleus of its thrust to regain dominance. The SAMs would be linked to key retailers to form a synergistic partnership of companies.

But why would a carpet mill want to develop a strategic alliance with the fiber manufacturer? What benefits would accrue to the mill by having a single yarn source? The company asked the mills these questions.

Part IV   Developing the SAMs Concept

Of the many carpet mills, eight controlled 46.8 percent of the market (the median market share in this fractionated business is only 2.25 percent). The company concentrated on those eight mills first. It set the following criteria for qualifying the mills as potential strategic partners:

● trust;
● attitude and philosophy;
● investment in their enterprise;
● competitive position;

- improvement potential for the fiber manufacturer.

Among these criteria, trust is the least quantifiable. It came down to polling the management as to their individual comfort level with the relationship to date—"the chemistry."

Attitude and philosophy was measured in terms of which mills were quick (inventory turns), lean (sales/employee), and clean (SG&A as a percent of sales. This refers to the sales, general and administrative costs, which measures the costs of organizational hierarchy relative to sales volume.)

Investment strategy indicated a willingness to grow with the fiber manufacturer as they jointly captured more market share. Conversely, a mill that would not invest in capacity before it absolutely needed to would quickly destroy the "virtual company" concept precisely when that capacity was needed to meet increased demand.

Measures of inventory as a percentage of net book value, or plant, property, and equipment (PP&E) and depreciation as a percent of net PP&E were employed as indicators of investment strategy.

Plotting market share percent against compound annual growth (CAG) of sales percent gave an indication of relative competitive position. Obviously, the company was looking for the bulls (and future bulls) in the industry.

A comparison of the mills' market share and the fiber company's sales to a mill as a percentage of its total sales introduced a potential dilemma: whether to target as potential SAMs those mills with high current penetration and reasonable market share or low penetration but high market share. In the end, the company chose as its SAM partners those mills it already had higher penetration with regardless of the mill's relative market share, reasoning that synergy would be easier built where the relationship was already more fully developed (getting back to the trust issue).

Profitability by customer was not a major consideration, since the logic was that premium servicing in the future would yield premium pricing. Furthermore, achieving the five-day vision would require a leaner organization and thus lower costs for both partners.

The company's analysis led to the choice of a pilot SAM that had a CAG more than double the industry median and a reasonable market share—one-third higher than the industry median.

Part V   Selling the Pilot SAM

A 1984 study found that only 14 percent of sampled U.S. manufacturers were employing Just-in-Time techniques. (In 1991 82 percent said they employed JIT techniques.) Of those companies that in 1984 used JIT techniques, nearly three-quarters said that their suppliers could supply them daily and that without JIT they could not take advantage of the supplier's level of excellence; in other words, customers were "forced" to improve their operations to improve the overall supply chain.

Basing its decision on that study, the fiber manufacturer concluded that it could form a "sales" approach to get a carpet mill to become the pilot SAM. The concept was that where both the fiber manufacturer and the carpet mill had high market share in both product and geography (shown in Figures 5.13 and 5.14), they could improve both mix and margin to their best customers by providing JIT-type deliveries. In areas where they both had low share they could gain by joint merchandising. Finally, in those areas where one had high share and the other low, the stronger would promote the weaker.

In addition to the market growth potential, the fiber manufacturer determined that there were other benefits to the carpet mill:

- Increased cash flow because the mill would pay the fiber company only after it had made the carpet and shipped to the retailer. (This looks like consignment inventory until it is realized that the mill receives dyed yarn eight hours at the most from the time it weaves the carpet.)

Selling More High-End Styles

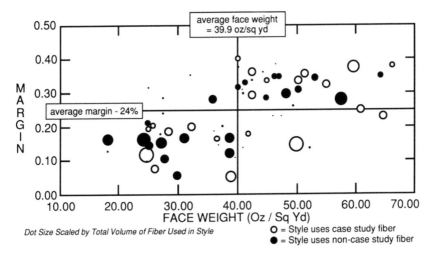

Figure 5.13 *Improving mix.*

Focusing Efforts

*On a Carefully Targeted Retail Population Will Enable
Results Quickly*

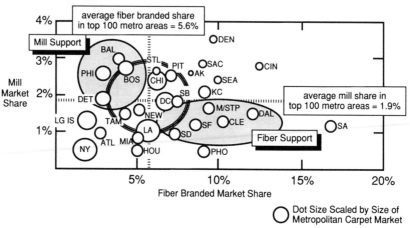

Figure 5.14   *Improving margin.*

- Inventory reduction of 48 percent and associated cost reduction of $16 million.
- Customer service levels of 99 percent vs. the current 65 percent.
- Rapid changeover would improve current equipment utilization by as much as 50 percent on some machines, realizing a direct labor capacity improvement equivalent to $1.2 million.
- Reducing cost of quality by $8 million (about 30 percent) by making to order with pre-dyed yarn, eliminating obsolescence, and saving some inspection costs.
- The new layout at the carpet mill would save $460K in eliminated material handling and accounting activity.

The clincher was that for the whole supply chain, every day of lead time reduction would realize a one-time positive cash flow of $520K (better than $50 million by reducing lead time by 15 weeks, or 105 days).

Part VI   Going Forward Together

The first mill the company approached agreed to pursue the concept of "virtuality". The two companies formed two joint task forces: one concentrating on lead time reduction and the other on marketing.

Each team was charged with developing and executing a plan. The teams began their work in mid-1992. By the end of 1992 the marketing team had determined that dealers were anticipating benefits to themselves and their customers.

Lead-time Reduction Team

Operational improvements that were required included some rationalization of product lines (the team determined that one-week service should be concentrated on the 10 percent of the product lines that yield 52 percent of the mill's volume). (See Figure 5.13.)

Goals were set to reduce the average changeover time from 4 hours to 15 minutes; to improve downtime by as much as 50 percent; to reduce the cost of quality; and to rearrange the factories to accommodate process flow. In order to realize these improvements, the companies would have to develop training modules for how to accomplish them and, as importantly, why the two companies were trying to realize these improvements.

Both companies had to rethink their scheduling philosophies and systems. The fiber company had a monthly push schedule to forecast and the mill had a weekly or daily pull schedule in orders (distribution center forecasts and/or replenishments). There were disconnects between forecasting and yarn scheduling, yarn production and tufting, and retail demand and distribution center orders to the factory.

Work-in-process tracking was cumbersome, uninformative, time consuming, and unnecessary once the throughput time was reduced to hours rather than weeks. The companies also had to develop a computer networking *cum* scheduling system that spanned the entire supply chain. That network came to be known as CARPETNET.

Marketing Team

This team reviewed the market share data, assessed other metrics such as local economy, the effectiveness of company personnel assigned to the area, market preference, etc. (See Figure 5.14.)

The team assigned one metropolitan area for prototyping and formulated a joint sales program. At the same time, it identified dealer BreakPoints throughout the marketplace.

Specifically, the team determined that cost and speed were the two BreakPoints, and that the carpet mill's quality and reliability were considered a price of entry.

Training programs were developed for the dealers on how to hook into and use CARPETNET.

As 1993 began, a dealer network was becoming firmly established and by the end of the year, the companies were expecting to see a marketplace reaction.

6
The New Assets

To many, assets mean capital or wealth, and their acquisition is regarded as an important measure of business performance. But increasingly, business people are coming to recognize that assets mean more than financial strength and include all of the resources at the disposal of the business. While financial executives, accountants, and auditors still talk about assets as cash, cash equivalents, and tangible items that depreciate, any operations executive will say that he has many non-cash assets in his portfolio.

In the new way of process orientation, what we call the "new assets"—these non-cash assets—take on extra importance. Successful process management manages the new assets rather than actively managing the old assets. And by actively, indeed aggressively, managing the new assets, successful process-oriented companies *de facto* manage the old assets.

These assets include people, product and process knowledge and capabilities, the strength of the company's brands, and the contents of information data bases. Under current accounting standards, some of these non-financial assets can be given a monetary value—albeit a very conservative one— while others are lumped at the point of acquisition or merger into the notion of "goodwill."

Far from being intangibles, the power of bonds of branding (brand equity in the United States), for example, is evidenced in that every consumer will pay more for Coca-Cola than for a local brand of cola, even when he or she cannot distinguish which is which in a blind tasting.

It is not surprising, therefore, that there is a constant tension between the accountant—the valuer of financial assets—and the operations executive—the orchestrator who believes that he should invest to enhance the value of all his assets. Cutting-edge leaders of businesses today concentrate more on the new assets than the old, while the operations executive today spends three to five times more effort on the new assets than a decade ago.

It is common business practice today to trade in the new assets. Patents can be traded in technological joint ventures such as those encouraged by the European Communities' Sprint Program, which was set up by the European Community to aid in the transfer of technology between businesses and nations. It is funded by national governments and provides grants and information to businesses and technology transfer networks such as brokers and universities throughout the European Community.

Information itself can be sold as a commodity and often is between mail order businesses, or by publishers who target telemarketing campaigns to those who have attended seminars or bought a book about a particular subject. Brands can be bought and sold without the sale of the company that owns them, as in the Cadbury, Schweppes, Coca-Cola deals. In his book, *World Class Brands*, Chris Macrae recalls an interview with Sir Adrian Cadbury in April 1989, two months before his retirement as Chairman of Cadbury Schweppes (a post he had held for 14 years).

> "The eighties were a period of accelerating change in the life of Sir Adrian's Company. This stemmed from the management conviction that horizons like Europe's open market signalled the beginning of an era which would increasingly benefit companies with a worldwide focus. Several businesses were sold (including the food division to a management buy out team) so that Cadbury Schweppes could practise a two-pronged ambition to be in the world's top divisions in both confectionery and soft drinks. As famous brands became increasingly fashionable, the company had to employ all its strengths to keep clear of hostile bid makers who were rumoured to be shimmering for a conquest.
>
> "Sir Adrian believed that to compete internationally in the nineties, a company could not afford to be in the second division of a branded

marketplace. Confectionery now has five world class players: Nestlé, Mars, Cadbury, Hershey and Jacobs Suchard. Being one of the leaders matters. Being one of them to Sir Adrian gives you the credentials to invest in the latest technology, to continue to attract the best people, to deal as an equal with the trade and to be respected for independent corporate values in the joint ventures you enter."

In the old way of doing business the accountants still seem to hold sway. "Remember Rolls Royce," is their rallying cry. "It capitalized the R&D costs of the RB211 engine then failed to make the predicted sales. The stock market didn't value the business at the same level the executives did. The resulting crash led to bankruptcy and a government bailout." From this is derived the accounting axiom: "Don't let companies give any real value to non-physical or non-financial assets."

But in many ways it is the financial assets and not the new assets that have little value to the business. They only measure its performance for the stockholder.

The new productive assets, on the other hand, are used in all kinds of business processes and translate into productive capabilities. In the new way of doing business, *all* assets are considered to have a value, and must be carefully managed. Investments must be made in non-physical and non-financial assets to assure their continued quality and that they remain state-of-the-art. Business performance measures must be created that recognize the value of these assets and the need to invest in their improvement.

Writing in *The Times* (London) on 1 October 1992, Keron Bhattacharya, author of *Accountancy's Faulty Sums*, argued that:

"Figures rarely determine a company's value. That is why some companies in the stock market sell at multiples of annual earnings two or three times the competitor's or market capitalization far in excess of capital employed. We all know why. Perhaps the company can boast dynamic management, dominant market share, a competent cooperative workforce, high R&D spending and enviable customer satisfaction ... These are not items you find on the balance sheet."

Business executives must work to convince their shareholders that if the new assets are managed properly, they will produce a financial profit. In fact, managing the process that manages the new assets effectively will remove the need to aggressively manage the old assets, and that only by maximizing the return on all of the new non-financial assets can the financial assets of the company be maximized in the long term.

For example, look at an investment in training. It has long been regarded as sound business sense to educate and train staff. Well-trained staff will operate more effectively and efficiently, thus increasing the organization's performance in its market. Yet, such an investment cannot be seen to contribute directly to profitability. Indeed, it is a direct cost that will reduce profits.

Few business leaders have been able to see beyond the short-term costs of training to the long-term increase in corporate abilities. But even in times of recession, corporate downsizing, and searching for ways to cut costs, leaders should ask what is going on and not be elated when they see reduced spending on training!

Some highly successful companies have ignored the figures and understood that investments in training are essential. In IBM, for example, there exists a skill's matrix whereby a line operator can grow in depth or breadth, depending upon the individual's choice. IBM is willing to give as much as 20 percent of a worker's time to that effort, and is willing to pay more in the pay check once the skills are acquired.

Motorola has invested in Motorola University, where state-of-the-art technologies are taught to *every* employee. To demonstrate the strategic value that Motorola places on its university, the senior vice president in charge reports directly to the CEO.

Too often, the old definition of assets drives companies blindly to cut costs. The new definition of assets, however, drives companies to add value to their assets to enhance revenues. Shareholders need to understand that whether the new assets are acquired or home grown, they will not appear instantly on the balance sheet, but rather they will appear over time in better long-term financial health.

The essential issues for management in the new era are as follows:

1 If a company does not maintain the new assets, it will not be able to manage and control core business processes.

2 Once the new assets have been identified, a company must recognize that they can be bought and sold like any physical or financial asset.
3 The new assets must be made to work, and a return is expected from this activity.

The third of these issues for managers provides the link between the new assets and Business Process Reengineering. Assets of all types are used in business processes. Maximizing the use of assets and generating a return on their use has long been the principal task of management. There is no difference in the new way of working; only that the number of assets to be considered has increased.

Clearly, when a process is reengineered it will often lead to a change in the way that the assets are allocated and used in the process. Therefore, to successfully reengineer either core or supporting business processes, managers must invest in and measure the performance of their new assets. They must develop algorithms and systems for their allocation and capacity control. Finally, they must develop the ability to communicate the logic of their actions to the community of external observers, who will otherwise judge harshly their seemingly illogical behavior.

UNDERSTANDING OF THE NEW ASSETS IS JUST BEGINNING

We are just beginning to see this new understanding of assets coming into being in the way companies hunt for merger or acquisition candidates. For some time, companies have been buying other companies specifically to acquire particular brands, for example RJR bought Del Monte and Nabisco, and Suchard bought Rowntree Mackintosh. Although brands are an intangible asset, they have always had a value placed on them.

But only recently have companies gone deeper into the list of intangible assets and looked to acquire such assets as core competence, technology, and processes. These assets not only provide new products and market access, but they can be leveraged into other areas of the company.

For instance, the Swiss camera and instrumentation manufacturing company, Leica, bought the smaller U.K. scientific
instrument and microscope maker, Cambridge Instruments,
for its entrepreneurial management team, which was then
installed at the head of Leica. And large pharmaceutical companies, especially German and Japanese, are gobbling up small
U.S. biotechnology companies not just for product but for
process knowledge.

Until shareholders learn how to value the new assets,
companies will continue to be very cautious about balancing
the short-term and long-term implications of expenditure.

The U.K. company BTR Group has attempted to take over a
number of companies in search of process knowledge. One
was Pilkington, with its float glass processes. Pilkington had
invested a lot of money on its process technologies, which was
not reflected on its balance sheet. BTR attempted to buy the
company at its depressed market value, but was rebuffed, at
great cost and drain on the focus of executives of both
companies.

In the case of Leica and Cambridge Instruments, a group
on the board of directors voted out the old Leica executives
who sat on the board and voted in the entire Cambridge
Instruments team.

In the U.S., the BTR Group tried to take over the Norton
Company, a maker of abrasives, for its process knowledge.
Norton turned to the French company, St Gobain, as its
"White Knight." St Gobain, in turn, recognized that Norton's
ceramic technology was superior to its own, picked Norton
clean of its intangible assets and, over time, installed its own
board of directors along the way.

This entire process prompted the legislature in Massachusetts to create a state law as a poison pill against BTR.
Under this law, only one-quarter of a company's directors can
be replaced in any three-year term, which effectively forces
companies to take 12 years to complete a takeover and install
a totally new board. Although St Gobain was willing to take
the time and create a relatively stable transition, this law has
served to keep other companies from attempting to take over
companies incorporated in Massachusetts and, especially
during the recession of the late 1980s and early 1990s, kept

capital from flowing into the state and possibly helping to lessen the effects of the bad economy; companies closed instead of being taken over.

In time it is likely that investors, regulators, and even legislators will come to understand that it is not only physical assets that have a value in a business. Such understanding is vital if business is to be conducted over the long term and every expenditure decision is not to be made on the basis of its likely impact on today's stock market price.

Businesses must take a long-term view of their investments in R&D, training people and installing information systems since they often take many years to provide a tangible financial return. The stock market though can react in minutes. Fear of a hostile takeover cannot be allowed to inhibit sensible long-term investment in new assets.

CAPACITY PLANNING

In order to manage new assets effectively it is essential that their provision is carefully planned and that their deployment is carefully controlled. The bridge between available assets and the business processes in which they are used is capacity management.

In the old way, resources were pushed at the business. First, a sales forecast was created. Then a rough guess was made to assess the business's requirements in terms of physical assets, people, plant, working capital for materials, etc. Then production was pushed to create product at the level of the forecast demand.

It was even common in many capital goods businesses to create a kind of contract between the sales and manufacturing functions to institutionalize the approach. Under the contract, manufacturing would undertake to flex output by +/− 10 percent annually. If the market dropped below this level, then the goods would be dispatched anyway. Such contracts drove Japanese marketers to seek foreign markets for their excess goods, creating new markets for Japanese companies in the diesel engine and earth moving vehicle markets.

The new way begins with assessing market demand, which then places a certain demand on the core business processes. This demand causes the core business processes to operate at a certain level, which in turn determines what assets are needed. The assets required lead to a plan for resources (people, materials, etc.).

This kind of flexible demand-driven resource loading will be familiar to those who have worked with Just-In-Time production methods. In this approach, a uniform plant load (UPL) is set. This load, or rhythm, determines the rate at which resources are provided to the plant and the rate of output of finished product. The essential point of UPL, however, is that because it is uniform, while variations in demand still exist, variations in the demand on resources are negligible.

Supporting processes are treated like assets and get pulled to the core process as required. A supporting process might be the provision of computer processing power for the manufacturing operation. A contract might be negotiated with a services company to supply the computing power necessary rather than the company purchasing a piece of capital equipment, which has a capacity limit.

The Mars Company has driven down the number of employees and driven up the revenue per employee by contracting for the services of everyone who does not manufacture candy bars. The company uses as performance measures, revenue per employee, and return on total assets (ROTA); these measures tend to drive the business to subcontract all processes except the core business processes.

Let us look closely at an example of how assets are pulled to a core business process. The company in question is a manufacturer of diesel engines. The core business process is new-product development, and successful market launch. One process within this core business process is designing cylinder heads.

The assets necessary for this process are many. There are the human assets, including a thermodynamics specialist, a mechanical engineer, a manufacturing engineer, technicians, draftsmen, and others. Other assets are needed, including computer-aided design (CAD) and computer-aided engineering (CAE) workstations and software. To design efficiently, drawings are needed on previous developments. Finally, buildings to house the design team and some money to pay them are required.

These assets will be drawn into the process as it proceeds. Take the thermodynamics specialist, he will be required at the beginning of the process to prepare rough sizing of the cylinders. Later he will be required to conduct detailed heat-flow calculations on the cooling circuit. The specialist has a very variable work load, and in the long run the business is only likely to need one specialist. However, the core business process is measured by cost, service, quality, and speed; thus it might be necessary to have two or more specialists in order to meet these performance criteria.

This would seem to be vast overprovision of thermodynamic specialist resources to the core business process. One might ask: why not outsource such specialized engineering?

But one can justify this apparent extravagance when one considers the whole process. The product gets to market sooner, thus giving a faster return on development investment and longer periods of profitability before competition catches up. Also, a company never wants to sacrifice technical capabilities that are part of the core business process (such as thermodynamic engineering) to a subcontractor; rather, the company can save far more and eliminate huge layers of support by contracting out such services as information technology, facilities management, etc.

The process of designing cylinder heads within the core business process has subprocesses linked to it. One such subprocess is establishing the process capability for valve-guide reaming. This process, in turn, pulls to it both human and non-human assets. This series of processes within the core process can be visualized as shown in Figure 6.1. Such processes are generally considered as part of the core business process rather than as a supporting process, since they are processes in their own right which determine the product's success.

There are, none the less many supporting processes that enhance the effectiveness of the core business processes.

Providing CAD equipment is an important supporting process in designing cylinder heads. Assets for this supporting process include money to purchase, maintain, and install CAD

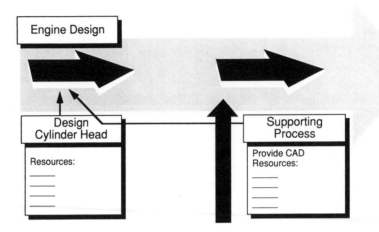

Figure 6.1   Core Business Process: New Product Development.

workstations, technicians to set up the equipment at the design team's location, training support for engineers and designers, etc.

Another supporting process for the designing of cylinder heads is providing quality and experimentation techniques and knowledge. Assets here include a quality engineer, manufacturing engineering, computer equipment, a body of technical knowledge, and data from manufacturing about its capabilities.

Capacity planning must be carried out at the overall business level to cover all of the core business processes, with demand calculated for the various assets and resources consumed in all the core processes, supporting processes, and subprocesses. The assets needed for diesel engine design are different for a company that designs one new engine a year than for a company that designs one new engine every four years.

Since supporting processes are pulled as needed by the core business process, there must be enough supporting resources to be pulled on an infinite basis. No core business process should be prevented from achieving its performance targets by a lack of supporting resources.

This approach, however, can lead to inefficiencies, with a lot of assets used in supporting processes idle at one time and every asset utilized at another. This dilemma, in turn, is leading more and more companies to subcontract support processes. Why own 50 CAD workstations when 50 are needed for two months a year but only 28 are needed the rest of the year? Why create an enormous data processing bureaucracy if that is not a core business process?

The bottom line is: *Do not let supporting processes become a bottleneck to the core business process.*

Indeed, companies left and right are shedding their data processing departments, and companies like IBM are spinning off service businesses to run them. Rosenbluth Travel in the United States or Hogg Robinson in the United Kingdom will locate an office on a client's site, doing away with the necessity for a corporate travel support process. Airlines have gone out of the food preparation business for the most part, and companies like Marriot, originally in hotels, have created entire divisions to supply airline meals. Reebok, the shoe company, has determined that its core business processes are marketing and design, and has contracted out all manufacturing. The list goes on.

A focus on core business processes often brings with it a wave of strategic alliances, which can lead to the condition we call "virtuality." This is particularly the case in defense industries where there is a real need to spread and to share risk. In the defense industries it is becoming very expensive to develop new products and the U.S. DoD increasingly requires business itself to fund developments.

With a broader definition of assets and a more hands-on approach to managing those assets, capacity balancing becomes important.

In the old way of doing business, a company takes orders and places them into the current capacity. In the new way, a resource manager moves resources backwards, forwards, within or across processes, balancing resources of different types over time. In very large businesses there is even an opportunity for computerized asset management. This subject is addressed in more detail in Chapter 7.

Resources may move with a product through the process, or they may be utilized in a more specific way. For instance, in Philips Medical Systems, some members of each product-development team move with a product from conceptual science all the way through to in-hospital customer service. At some companies that work this way, areas of expertise such as manufacturing engineering become a technical consulting group—hence a support process—to the new product-development group. The manufacturing engineering group is much smaller than when it was a discreet function, since many former members are now on product-development teams that follow the entire process.

At AT&T Power Systems, described in Chapter 3, all members of former functions that fed into new product design now sit on design teams and work on custom power sources, drawing the next request for a design out of the hopper and working through from concept to prototype. AT&T, which used to take weeks or months to respond to a customer's request for a design proposal, now strives to respond in three days.

One of the major goals in this effort, of course, is to move as much as possible toward variable cost processes with minimal fixed assets. These are processes that can expand or shrink as demand requires, with resources, especially people, who can flow into and out of as many processes as possible.

One inevitable outgrowth of accepting process orientation will be excess resources. The resource manager will have to determine what to do with unneeded or obsolete physical and human capacity.

Options for what to do with excess people include vertical integration; i.e. bringing back either upstream or downstream work that has been previously farmed out; increasing maintenance activity; creating problem-resolution teams; even giving workers to the city or county for the duration of their employment. What is clear is that once the process is reengineered, excess people must be moved out of the business, or the tendency will be to create new inefficiencies just to keep people busy.

Even for those who maintain their employment, a shift to a process-driven culture can be harrowing, as will be discussed in greater detail in Chapter 8. As people move through the process, they begin to lose their functional ties; their job changes as they move over time through a process or across processes. Some thrive on the constant challenge and learning, but clearly many feel lost and insecure.

THE NEW ASSETS AND MEASUREMENT

How does a company measure the new assets? It certainly requires new ways of thinking. For instance, today research teams are often measured by learned-papers written in the fields of the company's product development. In the new way, they will be measured more by how much of their R&D is commercialized.

When the assets are well developed and well utilized in order to enhance core business processes, the reengineered core processes in effect "kick back" and enhance the value of the assets. The circle begins again. In other words, getting a better process directly enhances the value of the assets that make up the process.

Enhancing the value of the new assets is the real job of operations executives. The COO must liberate the operations executives to manage operations in a way that will enhance long-term value instead of chasing pseudo effectiveness in the short term for the benefit of the stock markets.

For example, British Petroleum's core business processes are exploration and refining. Continually developing the assets necessary for these core processes has developed many technical capabilities. BP could just sit on these capabilities, but instead it chose to use them to create new business opportunities through BP Ventures, a separate business whose aim was to turn non-core activities in to revenue generating businesses in their own right. Today, BP is the largest producer in the world of solar cells, and has developed and marketed, a catalyzer system for flaring off gases at refineries.

Brands and Image

Let us look at a brand or a corporate image as an asset. Increasing the efficiency of the brand or image enhancement supporting process can lead to an increase in brand or company recognition. So can the recognition that comes from improving processes and gaining public recognition for doing so. This might be from winning the Baldrige or Shingo Award, or any other award.

The U.S. General Accounting Office has determined that companies that win the Commerce Department's Malcolm Baldrige Award for quality receive a 13.7 percent market share improvement in the next few years, and an 8.6 percent improvement in sales per employee.

The Allen-Bradley company built a "lights out" facility in Milwaukee, Wisconsin, to manufacture European specification motor starters. The company used the U.S. model motor starters to run the facility. The use of the company's own product to create the efficient manufacturing process in turn created corporate name recognition for the European products. Allen-Bradley realized that in order to penetrate the European market while making the product in the United States, it had to do something spectacular right from the beginning. The company developed this fully automated assembly line, which at the time was one of the first in the United States. The company also put on a public relations push; executives would go anywhere, speaking at any forum, just to push the message that the company had created a state-of-the-art system to manufacture European motor starters, which not coincidentally featured the company's U.S. motor starters.

Wal-Mart has done much the same thing with its "always low prices."

And Tom's of Maine, which makes toiletries such as toothpaste, looks for increased corporate and brand recognition by packaging all products in environmentally safe containers and manufacturing with all natural ingredients. The company advertises environmental tips, not the benefits of its toothpaste, and constantly researches new environmentally friendly products and processes. The company's advertising tag line is: "We compete with our values."

Process Technology and Knowledge

Many companies have used knowledge or intellectual property to enhance their core business processes. The following examples may give other businesses ideas for the exploitation of the new assets.

Digital Equipment Corporation created VAXnotes software,

a worldwide computer-based conferencing system for DEC product developers. The system, which was designed to improve the product development process, has an architecture such that a researcher can enter and take part in one of a number of conferences, query to see who is interested in the same issues as he or she is, split off from a conference and form a sub-conference, etc. DEC makes the VAXnotes software available to preferred clients for their own product development efforts.

Sometimes a breakthrough in the use of intellectual property can lead to a BreakPoint in the marketplace. In order radically to improve its delivery reliability in the custom lighting fixture market, as was discussed in Chapter 5, on BreakPoints, Lithonia lighting created an expert system that captured and structured the knowledge of its process and product experts for use by other less experienced and less knowledgeable individuals.

Process technology knowledge can also be a highly valued asset. Cummins Engine worldwide drills holes in cast iron better than any other company. In Gloucestershire, U.K., another engine manufacturer, Lister Diesels, spent 18 months intensively defining its manual processes in order to create a layout for a robot system that became a technical breakthrough.

On the old machining line, men loaded a casting on to a machine at each step of the machining process. On the redesigned U-line, fully automated with a pull system, a robot in the centre moved the casting from one machining operation to another. It took two months to design the line, four months to receive the automation equipment, then 18 months to transfer the process knowledge from the human machinists and get the robot to "understand" how to perform the tasks successfully.

For instance, when a man put the casting block on to a machine, he twisted it so it would fit into place correctly. But when the robot put the block down and it did not go right into place, the line would stop. But once the robot "learned" the little human tricks of the trade, it got every block into place on every operation so true that the company now produces the finest honed cylinder bore in the world, so fine that the engine does not have to be run in, it can start up and run right away to operate at full efficiency.

People

People really are a company's most important asset. Some companies have recognized the value of people to the extent that they have created entire lines of business around the skills their people develop over time.

Tennant, the maker of floor-sweeping products, created such an effective sales force through the application of Total Quality techniques and workforce empowerment, that it went on to develop an entire business in training other companies in quality and participative management techniques.

The electric utility company Florida Power and Light was so successful in the mid-1980s in its TQM efforts—it won the prestigious Deming Award from the Japanese Union of Scientists and Engineers—that it also began a TQM consulting practice. FPL created the concept of the "golden thread" and the rigorous seven-step process of taking an end goal—often process oriented —and breaking down that goal to its elements, then breaking down each element to its sub-elements. For instance, the goal of providing customers with better service has, among others, the elements of quality, empathy, and lead time.

Although FPL no longer applies this rigorous process within its business, this is due more to its obsession with TQM at the expense of other initiatives than to any inherent fault in the company's strategy.

Clearly, in terms of people, the big challenge for both line managers and senior management is to know what effects changes to a process orientation will have on people. In a process-oriented company, people will be identified, measured, rewarded, and promoted not by seniority but by the skill sets they possess, their intellectual and problem solving capabilities, and their competence in understanding and improving the process, and their ability and willingness to be team players and contributors. The shock that this brings, particularly to those who are pursuing other career goals, can be dramatic.

Information

The information companies possess has enormous value. The

raw data is itself an asset, as are the processes the company employs to organize that data and create information, which confer on that data added value. How that information is organized and marshalled can create competitive advantage. And the further upstream and downstream a company can go to collect and then integrate the data, the more chance there will be to enhance its core business process.

For instance, automobile companies have for 20 years been using a system called broadcasting, in which data is sent upstream from the assembly operation to the suppliers as to what configuration of parts is necessary to produce the next sequence of cars to roll off the line.

Similarly, the Coca-Cola Company gets point-of-sale data from retail outlets, at least theoretically, when each bottle is purchased. By getting the data upstream to suppliers of bottles, caps, and labels, the company can closely manage its materials and capacity, and produce exactly the right soft drink at the time demanded by the market. Wal-Mart has created a similar information flow with its suppliers.

How companies store their data can also have an effect on processes. In the product-design area, for example, Western companies tend to collect data and store it in a large data base within one computer located in the middle of the engineering department. This computer requires a separate supporting function to run it, and forces a centralized discipline on the designers who have to work with the system. Japanese companies, on the other hand, tend to collect and store their data at each step of the process: their data bases mirror the process flow.

Because of the rapid growth in computer technology since the 1960s and the way in which many people have become enamored with that technology, there has arisen a confusion in many managers' minds between information and information technology.

Information technology is an enabler; it helps transmit, manipulate, and present information in a useful way. However, it is the information itself that is the useful asset. Information is the new asset that has value and can be used to enhance the core business process's performance. The hardware and software that constitutes information technology is just one of the old physical assets. It is only worth what the market will pay for it.

However, information must often be organized so as to enhance a core business process, and information technology is often important in effecting that organization.

Larry Bossidy, the CEO of Allied Signal, says the speed of his managers' ability to make process decisions will be one of the competitive advantages his company has, and that gathering, organizing, and making available information will be one of the key enablers of those managers' decisionmaking ability. Making the technology work to gather, organize, and make available the right information to the right managers, in turn, is the technological key to enhanced process capability.

As another example, the Bank of Boston used to use six different systems and computers to pass a cancelled check. By consolidating its systems and creating a single data base the bank now can clear a check in 20 percent of the previous time and thereby better manage the money float to its advantage.

VALUING AND MANAGING THE NEW ASSETS

It is clear from the above that accounting standards and approaches do little to help in the valuation of the new assets. However, in order to defend investments and to report coherently to shareholders, it is important for the business-person to place value on assets.

Just like physical assets it should be remembered, the new assets depreciate over time, and must constantly be developed, enhanced, renewed, and regenerated. It is hard to determine the return to the company of developing, enhancing, renewing, and regenerating non-tangible assets, while at the same time it is relatively easy to determine the monetary cost. This makes it hard for executives to justify the costs.

An executive can say, "we need to maintain state-of-the-art process knowledge in order to assure continued excellent business performance." But the market analyst, accountant or shareholder will often reply, "Prove it. If you cut costs for training and education, conferences, and information systems you actually improve the bottom line?"

The executive must be able to argue cogently that the consequence of good management of the new assets will be *de facto* management of the old assets. Executives have for a long time been able to justify the cost of brand equity protection and advertising, both of which are very difficult to measure, as effective ways to assure long-term market position even though they are costs. The same line of reasoning can, and must, be used to argue for the enhancement of the new assets.

The executive must try to avoid the trap of justifying monetary investments on a stand-alone basis. Individual assets must be managed and measured in their own units of value, as well as in cost terms. Managers can give strong leadership to their teams by providing rough translations between the different measures of assets.

For instance, British Rail has a strategic goal to move towards zero accidents. The organization justifies investments in such efforts by creating a unit of safety performance that can be thought of as "equivalent lives saved." It has developed weightings, based on experience in other industries, to say that one unit of safety performance is equivalent to one death or ten major injuries and that one major injury is equivalent to ten minor injuries.

By making these management judgements British Rail has provided a powerful tool for its managers. It tells them that it will measure safety performance in terms of units of safety performance. It helps them to justify expenditure since it signals to managers the level of expenditure that it is prepared to accept in order to save an equivalent life.

This translation from units of safety performance to money enables the businesses that make up the railway to compare their investments in safety directly with their investments in more traditional assets such as track, signalling, and trains (often referred to as maintenance of way and maintenance of equipment). In other words, even though an investment of X million in new signals might not be justified as a way to speed travel between two points, when increased safety is considered, the combination of faster travel and better safety may, in fact, justify the cost.

IBM, Motorola, and a host of other companies justify their huge investment in training by arguing that people with flexible career paths give the company the ability to change strategic direction more rapidly, since they do not have to shed current employees and find new employees with new skill sets. This applies right down to the shopfloor. In Havant in Hampshire, UK, IBM employees earn promotion and recognition in accordance with the skill sets in which they have been trained.

CONTROL AND MANAGEMENT OF THE NEW ASSETS

It is important that the business, intent on following the new way of operating, should develop metrics that will enable it to measure its assets, these must include levels of investment and return. There are some useful metrics that can be employed to measure the new assets in the micro, while dollar value is used to measure the macro.

In the United Kingdom, a group headed by Sir Kenneth Corfield explored these issues in its study "Intangible Assets: Their Value and How to Report it." In that report, the group argued that, in the short term, the accounting profession needs to make modest steps to accept intangible assets as worthy of balance sheet valuation, but that accountants need to begin thinking today about more widespread overhaul of intangible-goods valuation for the twenty-first century. The report states:

> "Accounting should anticipate and accommodate rather than lag behind, and possibly impede, business development.
>
> "Examining the way forward to deal with the issues associated with intangible assets forces a refocus on the purpose of financial statements, which is essentially a report to shareholders on the performance of a business. Overworking the concept of prudence has militated against the usefulness of the financial statements. This balance needs to be redressed.
>
> "Insofar as intangible assets are concerned, values may be more difficult to determine, but unless they are reported in some way, it is difficult for shareholders to assess management's performance in

safeguarding and exploiting them. Throwing a spotlight on such assets ought, in turn, to heighten the need to control them effectively.

"A further thought on accountability to shareholders is that management is a custodian of value as well as existence and ownership. It is therefore unacceptable in responding to shareholder needs merely to flag the existence of intangible assets. Shareholders need to be made more aware of their value. That such values are subjective justifies greater disclosure of the nature of those assets and the way their values have been arrived at, rather than less disclosure and even total omission."

Measurement at the micro level is vital since the level of performance achieved in the use of the new assets will determine how well the old ones are managed. In this way, the executive can look the analyst, accountant or shareholder in the eye and say, "yes it costs money to do all of this, but look at the increase in capability and potential for the future."

Measuring the new assets should be done on an output basis, in their own units. For example, since information is an asset, a company should measure how up to date its data bases are, or the percentage of the available population that the data covers. If intellectual property is an asset in a particular company, then measures of new patents and successful commercialization may be relevant. By doing this, the company can measure effectiveness rather than efficiency. The team that is constructed and empowered to work on core processes will, by its very nature, deal with ineffective resources.

An analogy might be in flying a modern aircraft. Today's airplanes are built with such sophisticated avionics that the pilot does not have to manage all of the instrumentation, rather he concentrates on the macro and allows the plane (the process) to "fly itself" to a great extent.

The Japanese pokeyoke system works in much the same way, with operators responding to the exception and letting the process drive itself to the rule, rather than micro managing the process.

A key goal is to make the core processes as flexible as possible, and as variable cost driven as possible. Flexibility in resources allows as few fixed costs as possible to be allocated to the process. Furthermore, with flexible resources and low levels of fixed cost, most assets can be moved from one process to another as they are required.

The four key measures of core business process effectiveness are, of course, *cost, quality, time,* and *service.* These will be weighted differently for each core process.

If a company's management does not understand value and the need for investment in the development of the new assets, it simply will not be able to improve its core business processes or effect BreakPoints. The company will be stuck in the old paradigm, chasing world leaders or relegated to niches.

For large companies, the organizational challenges implied by the new way of working are especially formidable, and complicated by the need to convince shareholders and analysts of the long-term correctness of pursuing the new assets rather than rigidly focusing on maintaining high valuations in the traditional way.

7
Process Management in Large Businesses

As businesses enter the increasingly competitive world of the late twentieth century, they are using new methods to develop and compete. The central theme of management has become the customer, and value to the customer has become the unifying purpose.

Leaders and key managers of large companies are faced with the added complexities not only of size but of multiple location, and especially of needing to operate in many countries, when they seek to run their businesses in this new way. This chapter examines some additional tasks faced by management of large businesses, and presents the approaches used by some managements who have succeeded.

As businesses inevitably grow and move towards being global concerns, they have an opportunity to dominate their markets. Such domination will result not from using traditional economies of scale but rather from process orientation, from the combination of a focus on core business processes and a focus on providing value to the customer. Such an orientation implies that new supporting processes must also be created and applied.

These include early manufacturing involvement (EMI) teams, asset manager systems (probably computerized including artificial intelligence) for the new assets, new measures of performance, and new approaches to automation and motivation. Such a menu is rich meat to the leaders of businesses who would seek to "break the china."

To compete simultaneously at a national and global level, businesses must create superior value for the consumers of their products. This implies that they must engage in two new activities. They must understand what gives customer value and they must personally engage in the reengineering of their core business processes. The global business has opportunities to dominate markets where national plants are unable to penetrate.

For example, an automotive temperature controls manufacturer has several plants located throughout the world, each making essentially the same product line to the same specifications. Each plant, however, has its own distinct manufacturing method, each uses dissimilar equipment, and each inspects raw material according to different criteria. Some plants make to order and others make to stock.

As a result, products manufactured in one plant cannot be shipped to another plant's customers because of the varying performance characteristics, even though they are made to the same specifications. It has been estimated that by adopting a single global way of manufacturing, the company could realize a potential 36 percent reduction in the ex-works cost of goods.

Such a significant opportunity arises from the company's size and breadth. But to capture the opportunity, the company will have to become process oriented rather than function and nationality oriented. It will have to determine its core business processes, and reengineer them on a global scale; as well, it will have to redesign its local support processes.

Reengineering core processes in large multi-site and especially global organizations is clearly a more complex operation than reengineering core processes in a single-site business. However, as is so often the case in life, where the task is difficult the reward is correspondingly greater. Large businesses are provided an opportunity to exploit any Breakpoints to achieve global dominance in their target markets.

Take, for example, the economies of scale and scope that were exploited by the Japanese over two decades to take a commanding lead in the motorcycle, automotive, or consumer electronics markets. It has often been said that this dominance arises from marketing policies, product design, and export pricing policies. However, from the perspective of Business Process Reengineering, it is clear that this lead was, in fact, derived from a strong core process orientation and search for BreakPoints that could then be exploited to gain customer loyalty.

What constitutes a large business? For the purposes of this book, large businesses have more than one site from which essentially the same product categories or services are offered to the customer base. Such businesses often operate on a global scale and modify their products to suit local market traditions.

THE TREND TOWARD GLOBAL BUSINESS

The trend for businesses to become global is accelerating as new competitors appear to established businesses to be global rather than national. The goal of many businesses in globalizing their activities has become domination over the competition rather than merely to reach new markets.

Coopers & Lybrand's "Made in America III" study of manufacturing companies in the United States, conducted in 1991, found that companies' executives overwhelmingly believe global competition is affecting their businesses. Most also believe that globalization of their own business is inevitable.

The survey revealed that 78 percent of U.S. companies with $1 billion or more in sales currently produce more than 15 percent of their goods in other countries for sale in other countries. The percentage is projected to rise to 87 percent by 1996. In those companies with between $250 million and $1 billion of sales, the figures show a similar trend; 58 percent currently making and selling more than 15 percent overseas, and 72 percent predicted to be doing so by 1996.

Using this benchmark of 15 percent off-shore manufacture for off-shore sale as the definition of the "global" U.S. company, the survey showed that 77 percent of CEOs of global companies pay "a great deal of attention" to globalization issues. Even in "non-global" companies, 46 percent of CEOs regard globalization issues as important.

Between 74 and 82 percent of CEOs, depending on whether their companies are currently global or not, see globalization as the way of reaching markets worldwide.

Globalization is seen by its practitioners as part of their competitive advantage. Seventy-eight percent of CEOs of global companies see globalization as a way of gaining advantage over the competition, compared to only 55 percent of CEOs of non-global companies. This is the key finding of the survey, that the aggressive companies are globalizing (or furthering their globalization effort) because they want to dominate, not just compete or reach other markets. Truly they believe that leadership is ownership.

In the United Kingdom the scene is a little different. Manufacturing companies already see their competition as coming less from domestic U.K. companies and more from overseas competitors. Leaders of large manufacturing businesses surveyed in the 1992 Coopers & Lybrand "Made in the U.K." study say that in 1989 the major competitor for 53 percent of them was another U.K. company, and that by 1995 this would decrease to 36 percent. They see a slight increase in the number whose major competitor would be Japanese or American, from 6 to 8 percent and from 14 to 15 percent respectively over the same period. But the majority of these manufacturers consider their competition increasingly to be coming from companies based in the European Community, and predict that by 1995 22 percent of manufacturers will have as their major competitor a European company, compared to only 14 percent in 1989.

These two studies show that, although the definition of "global" competition may be somewhat different depending on the business context, businesses are increasingly feeling pressure from competition outside their traditional domestic competitors.

GLOBAL PROCESSES, BUT LOCAL CUSTOMERS

In order to be a successful global or pan-European competitor, companies need to create an environment that streamlines processes and creates as much commonality in product or service (and in process) as possible while maintaining the ability to respond to customer desires with both local and worldwide brands.

In his book, *World Class Brands*, Chris Macrae notes that brands seldom engender world class spirit without being sure of their own nationalities. There are two contrasting communications styles: one is an accepted stereotyping of a nation's image while steering clear of any national warts; the other tunes into a universal sense of excellence, which touches people irrespective of race or creed. Both types of brand aim to steer clear of issues concerning national passions.

The local brand is less concerned about its international image. In fact, it often protects its marketplace by playing on locally chauvinistic traits, which establishes its authority to identify with a local audience. Most worldly customers enjoy choosing between both kinds of experience. The global businesses that are analyzed here all exhibit remarkable dexterity in the handling of this local versus world class brand issue.

Customers around the world have common requirements. For example, they all need to wash their clothes. However, the methods they use may differ. For instance, in washing machines, Americans desire top loaders while the French and English like side loaders. The Italians prefer a short spin cycle, the Germans a long, vigorous spin cycle. But the basic technology and the core business processes of design and manufacture/assembly to make pumps, motors, agitators, drums, back guards, and pressed metal parts, are the same regardless of the final product configuration.

Likewise, the marketing messages needed to sell products may differ. An international company tried to market a detergent in Japan as being effective at all temperatures. The product was a disaster. Later research found that Japanese nearly always wash clothes in cold water, so the marketing message was irrelevant, despite its great appeal in other regions. A new marketing effort stressed the detergent's ability to work with the high levels of fabric conditioner the Japanese use, and the product was a major success.

Within the global enterprise there are constant tensions between centralization and decentralization, operating efficiency and marketing, economies of scale and local operations. Most large businesses have seen the possibilities of achieving economies of scale by consolidating their manufacturing operations. However, the local orientation of marketing has driven them inevitably to create different products in each market. Ultimately the situation becomes that of the temperature control company mentioned at the start of the chapter. Totally different standards exist at each operating location.

Over the years large businesses have been driven to begin operations in new sites for many reasons; ease of distribution, taxes and tariffs, political pressure for domestic content, even company expectations. Attempts are then made to transfer marketing between operations in the pursuit of economies of scale in the production of the good or service. Most of these efforts have been unsuccessful; the World Car and the Suchard European chocolate bar "Lilac" thus far both look like failures.

Both Unilever and Procter & Gamble worked hard to come out with a detergent concentrate. P&G developed it in one R&D center, and developed one worldwide product. Unilever, on the other hand, worked at 13 R&D centers and launched 13 products with even more packaging configurations. While the P&G product was more effective and had considerably lower development costs, the Unilever product outsold because of its recognition of local market packaging preferences.

GLOBAL REENGINEERING

Reengineering core business processes and achieving operational BreakPoints on a global scale can best be seen in Asea Brown Boveri (ABB). The stated goal and advertised proposition is, where possible, to drive the company toward global manufacturing and design, while at the same time maintaining close ties to local customers. This multifaceted business is what ABB's president and CEO, Percy Barnevik, calls a "multi domestic" enterprise.

ABB's more than 50 business areas, grouped into eight business segments, are worldwide in scale, with each business-area leader responsible for rationalizing and optimizing the business on a global scale. He is also responsible for maintaining worldwide cost and quality standards, and allocating export markets to each manufacturing facility. At the same time there is a national organization in each industrialized country in which ABB operates.

Within each of these national organizations there are usually subsidiaries for each of the business areas that operate in that country. Each country organization has its own structure and a career path exists within it for favored executives.

In this way, ABB has established more than 1100 companies that either manufacture, service, or sell the set of products from one business area in different countries. Presidents of each such company report to two people, the business-area president responsible for the product group sold worldwide, and the national president.

Barnevik put this in perspective for William Taylor, a *Harvard Business Review* associate editor, in a March/April 1991 interview. Taylor asked what a production worker in the ABB Combustion Engineering plant in Windsor, Connecticut, should feel no longer being part of an "American" company but rather a part of ABB's "federation." Barnevic responded:

"You should be happy as hell about it. A production worker in Windsor is probably in the boiler field. He or she does't care what ABB is doing with process automation in Columbus, Ohio, let alone what we are doing with turbines outside Gdansk, Poland. And that's fair. Here's what I would tell that worker: we acquired Combustion Engineering because we believe ABB is a world leader in power plant technology, and we want to extend our lead.

"We believe that the United States has a great future in power plants both domestically and on an export basis. Combustion represents 80 years of excellence in this technology. Unfortunately, the company sank quite a bit during the 1980s, like many of its U.S. rivals, because of the steep downturn in the industry. It had become a severely weakened organization.

"Today, however, the business is coming back, and we have a game plan for the United States. We plan to beef up the Windsor research center to three or four times its current size. We want to tie Windsor's work in new materials, emissions reduction, and pollution control technology in with new technologies from our European labs. That will let us respond more effectively to the environmental concerns here. Then we want to combine Combustion's strengths in boilers with ABB's strengths in turbines and generators and Westinghouse's strengths in transmission and distribution to become a broad and unique supplier to the U.S. utility industry. We also have an ambition for Combustion to be much more active in world markets, not with sales agents but through the ABB multi domestic network.

What counts to this production worker is that we deliver, that we are increasing our market share in the United States, raising exports, doing more R&D. That's what makes an American worker's life more secure, not whether the company has its headquarters in the United States."

ABB was created as the vehicle for Barnevik to exploit the considerable talents he had demonstrated in Sweden with Asea on a worldwide stage. The Brown Boveri group, once the pride of Swiss engineering, had become sleepy and was in decline.

Barnevik determined to pursue a simple strategy to achieve world dominance in selected markets. First, he bought as many competitors as possible in all the geographic markets of the world. Second, he set about rationalizing these businesses and introducing the Customer Focus Campaign. Finally, he has sought technological leadership through R&D and process developments.

The Customer Focus Campaign, started in 1990, concerned itself with the redesign and improvement of customer servicing processes, and was often subtitled: The Global Campaign for Time-Based Management and Total Quality Management (TBM & TQM). The origins of the quest for TBM & TQM are described below.

In 1990 ABB was competing in the power generation and distribution sectors, in environmental control equipment, and in rail transportation. These markets all were dominated by national interests, each country seeking to provide a flow of sufficient orders to its own ailing manufacturers.

The order-flow system itself was largely determined by the domestic economy of the host countries, and the level of domestic spending on infrastructure projects. Recognizing this feature of the chosen ABB markets and creating the concept of the "multi-domestic" strategy and the "global/local" company was a master stroke.

But Barnevik realized that after the massive acquisition phase, when the company grew to over 1200 companies, there was a need for consolidation and rationalization. It was inevitable that there would be duplications of activity and products, which ill-fitted the central product strategy.

He thus decided to base the rationalization efforts around process improvement focused on the customer. To begin this Customer Focus Campaign, Barnevik appointed a senior manager in the Orlikon, Zurich headquarters to lead a world-wide task force, which drew on the talents of some 40 senior managers from major operating countries around the world. The task force selected consultants to work with the operating companies, provided advice and information on appropriate tools and techniques to employ in the local process focus efforts, and issued regular briefings on the status of the efforts in each country and each company.

Each country-based or product-based company chooses its own way of going about the Customer Focus Campaign; each determines the core business processes that it needs to focus on in order to be more customer responsive, and where Break-Points might exist. All business unit CEOs have an objective on which they are measured in their annual appraisals and that is to run one full process-oriented project per year.

By the end of 1992 a number of BreakPoints had been explored, and some had been acted on, such as the manufacture of simple push buttons at a plant in Sweden, and the development and manufacture of power transformers in Secheron, which both employed Business Process Reengineering in order to reduce delivery lead time.

However, on a macro level, progress has been slow. Inevitably, because process orientation must take place at the business unit level, the responsibility for results lies with business unit leaders who have varying levels of skill and commitment to the undertaking, as well as other priorities they are measured against that sometimes conflict with process orientation.

Barnevik, for his part, spends much of his time reinforcing the message of the Customer Focus Campaign. He stresses that he is perfectly willing to do this; he says he is prepared to tell the same stories day after day.

Chapter 8 explores in greater detail the roles, responsibilities, and characteristics of the successful corporate and business unit leaders, as they embark on process orientation. The rest of this chapter focuses on the business activities central to creating process orientation in large companies.

CUTTING THROUGH TO PROCESSES IN LARGE BUSINESSES

As we have already said, large businesses that cross borders are not only complicated to manage, but while they have a number of special problems they are also full of opportunities to open up real competitive leads.

Market share has much more relevance in large than in small businesses. Large businesses often create elaborate competitive strategies, including the use of loss leaders to establish presence in a market or to injure the competition. Such activities require them to conduct sophisticated analysis in such areas as customer and competitor positioning.

Large businesses are often driven by elaborate budgeting that involves cross-subsidies between products and services, or between sites. Transfer pricing and transfer work mechanisms are developed to reap profits in countries where such profits are treated most favorably for tax purposes. It is possible to locate different or similar processes in different countries to take advantage of varying tax rules.

For instance, Ciba-Geigy does most of its pharmaceutical research in Switzerland, in order to generate profits in the country that can then be used to meet its corporate overheads. It charges its operating units around the world for these research efforts.

But companies should not get completely caught up seeking tax advantage; rather, they must consider the implication of taxes against process effectiveness and centers of excellence— the "can-do" vision elaborated in Chapter 5 on BreakPoints. Some businesses seem obsessed with minimizing taxes while others, much more appropriately, are looking to maximize global operational synergy.

This might entail creating worldwide R&D efforts that work round the clock and take advantage of talent wherever it is found. For example, when Philips Medical Systems set out to compete in the race to launch the world's first Nuclear Magnetic Resonance scanner, it operated a near 24-hour day research effort. In Digital Equipment Corporation, developers around the world keep in touch across time zones with the electronic mail systems and VAXnotes.

The organizational structure of large global businesses often involves units that are parallel in size, structure and geographic reach. However, there can be vast cultural differences between these units as they tend to develop their own cultural traditions in response to local markets and customs.

GLOBAL MANUFACTURING TECHNIQUES

As a business moves towards global status it will pass through a number of different forms. It is useful to examine these different forms in the context of a process-oriented view of a business, as they tend to determine the activities that must exist in the core business processes. Large businesses work in one of four forms:

1 National Manufacturing for Local Markets.
2 National Manufacturing for International Sales.
3 Multinational Manufacturing for International Sales.
4 Global Manufacturing.

National Manufacturing for Local Markets

In this form, a business, usually one that does not cross borders, uses a basic batch-oriented manufacturing approach, sometimes with islands of Just-In-Time or Automated Manufacturing Systems. Such businesses tend to have a perception of quality limited to the consistency of the product. They are unconcerned with design standards or consistency in design. Management often focuses on quick returns, which causes improvements to be task oriented rather than strategy driven.

National Manufacturing for International Sales

When selling internationally, a company's manufacturing is often the same as for local markets, but includes many more products to accommodate the demands of international buyers. Greater emphasis is placed on logistics control. Overall asset utilization, however, tends to be low. In general, quality standards are set by each host country while, for economies of scale, expansion in capacity is achieved on existing sites.

Figure 7.1 shows a single manufacturing facility supplying worldwide demand for pneumatic thermostats. Since demand for this type of device in all markets except the U.S. is relatively small, it makes no sense to manufacture elsewhere.

Multinational Manufacturing for International Sales

Operating like national plants but located at various sites throughout the world, multinational businesses make similar products that are customized to meet local requirements. Each site often has its own manufacturing approach. Most products and processes are developed locally. Multinational manufacturing has higher overall costs and is less effective in the use of global manufacturing assets than single-site operations. The duplication of effort usually results in the widespread duplication of support functions.

The multinational's plants are usually staffed by nationals whose culture differs from that of workers at sister sites or corporate headquarters. Diverse quality standards inhibit significant shipments of finished product from passing between sites. Technology transfer tends to be minimal because of

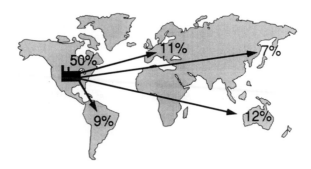

% Of Pneumatic Thermostats In Each Market

Figure 7.1   *Single plant sourcing (Pneumatic Thermostats).*

varying traditions and standards. Sourcing of capital equipment and systems is frequently locally inspired, and attempts to reconcile corporate and local driving forces often result in the use of inappropriate technologies.

Figure 7.2 shows the same company's production facilities for digital thermostats. With great demand throughout the world, there is a need for multiple plants. In theory, with low transportation costs, plants can produce for any geographic market, but are often inhibited by lack of product and process uniformity.

Business Process Reengineering within large businesses therefore often has as a goal the achievement of common approaches to manufacturing and, ideally, distribution in all of the company's worldwide operations. A focus on core business processes is particularly powerful in global businesses as it enables synergy to be obtained between operations. Core business processes can be identified and reengineered globally, while support processes can be redesigned at a local level to take advantage of local practices. In this way the global business can maintain the right feel for local and regional customers.

Shell International, for example, maintains a central Business Process diagram for the Lubrication businesses, to which all operating companies around the world are expected to conform. This high-level view of the core business processes is used to obtain efficiency in information systems investment,

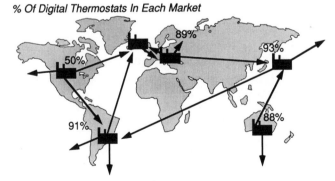

% Of Digital Thermostats In Each Market

Figure 7.2 *Multi-plant sourcing (Digital Thermostats).*

and to develop process technology that can be used in the different corners of the world.

Global Manufacturing

In the past, true global manufacturing has been confined to repetitive or process industries, as opposed to job shops or one-off manufacturers, and is still most easily accomplished in such an environment. In such industries, core business processes are easily transportable, and the core technologies, raw materials, and philosophies are universally recognized. The key processes usually do not require a high degree of manual dexterity, and are protected against failure with computers.

Most of the manufacturing complexity is in the process rather than in the product, although this is sometimes difficult to recognize "in the heat of battle" while getting the goods out the door every day. It is only when one goes through a visioning exercise that it is recognized that the process complexity can be managed and that product complexity can be easily managed.

For example, a PC manufacturer sold over 1000 configurations of 17 basic models. Product complexity justified extraordinary process complexity. It was only when the product design was analyzed that the manufacturer realized that it had designed excessive complexity into the product. For instance, one model had the mother board (PCB) at the bottom of the box and the power supply and hard disk above the PCB. In another model, the positions were reversed.

At a minimum, there were 17 different process routings. The unique designs precluded the company from employing a process assembly line where each fixed station was responsible for one or more subassemblies and insertions into the box.

After process redesign, the complexity could be managed using one basic process routing and a broadcast system similar to that successfully employed by automotive assemblers.

In the process industries to date it has been more common for knowledge of state-of-the-art technology to exist in one or at most two locations worldwide, and to be introduced only when a new product is to be launched simultaneously at all sites. The simultaneous introduction of new processes requires central quality standards and instrumentation, centralized purchasing of equipment, central risk management, and Early Manufacturing Involvement (EMI) teams.

EMI teams include personnel from each affected site and critical function, such as design and manufacturing engineering, quality assurance, service and maintenance, as well as key suppliers, who are responsible for the introduction of core technologies at each site. It is most important to provide a common language for members of staff when they meet to discuss their activities such as marketing or technical standards.

It is important to acknowledge the difference between process and service or discrete industries. The process industry tends to be more capital intensive, and therefore finds it harder to replicate manufacturing process globally, since each plant will come on-line at a different point in the technological maturity of the process.

Such difficulties do not mean that the customer service processes cannot be reengineered. For example, within the manufacturing process, changeover can be reengineered. In service or discrete companies, it is possible to mirror activities globally. These industries are people intensive and people are the most flexible of all resource types.

Figure 7.3 shows the same production configuration with added core business processes to manage assets in place. These

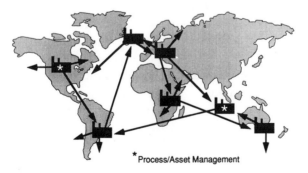

*Process/Asset Management

Figure 7.3   *Global manufacturing with asset management.*

processes make it possible to ship product of uniform quality and specification from any plant to any customer in the world.

In the global company, EMI teams are an important extension of the new-product or new-process development team. The aim of EMI teams is to acquire best practice in process application from anywhere in the world and then to apply it to every relevant facility in the world.

IBM was a pioneer in the use of EMI teams with the development of its cathode-ray tube (CRT) interfaces. Team members from each discipline at three manufacturing plants, located in Scotland, Japan, and the United States, met regularly. Development was done in any plant, with team members meeting each time there was to be a global roll out of a new innovation. At IBM the EMI team not only managed but *defined* the manufacturing and design rules.

In a global manufacturing business, labor costs are likely to be proportionately of little significance because of a low labor to automation ratio. Such businesses will exploit their dominance in the market to raise capital and technological barriers to entry, moving towards high levels of process automation, which in turn require careful attention to the core business processes.

For example, the PC manufacturer mentioned earlier considered relocating its German fabrication, assembly, and test operations to Ireland, where labor costs were 50 percent of German costs. But after product redesign and process reengineering that significantly reduced the total labor costs, the subsequent minimal labor savings realized by the relocation could not justify the moving costs and potential market disruption.

Shipping products between the markets of a global business in a timely manner requires an appropriate logistics strategy. Such strategies rely heavily on computer networks, communications protocols and simulation software to model the most favourable outcomes. The logistics processes are some of the most often reengineered to achieve BreakPoints, since they occur at the final stage of transfer of goods to the customer.

Although products often have many features to meet local tastes, the main manufacturing processes are frequently restricted to a few options. For example, the pan-European washing machine discussed earlier can be fabricated and assembled employing the same reengineering process at any plant site, regardless of its final destination. Such manufacturing processes can be more easily transferred between sites, and the product design process can be driven to adapt to the capabilities of the manufacturing processes.

In the plants of a multinational manufacturer (one with many independently operating units) attempts are constantly made to balance central management concerns with local market preferences. Exchange rates, political issues, and regulatory differences must be traded off against internal concerns for resource productivity return on fixed assets and material supplies. This is achieved by continually increasing or decreasing capacity at specific sites and subcontracting work where this is necessary to meet demand. In many multinationals, plants are actually encouraged to compete with each other for the right to manufacture a new product!

In a global manufacturing environment, with centrally managed processes and transferable products, external and internal concerns become far easier to manage as each site recognizes that it is part of achieving a common objective. Management energy is not wasted on maintaining the *status quo*, but rather is focused along the core business processes, and at serving customers wherever they may be in the world. In practice, a good process will be self-managing. Thus, management can concentrate more on the customer than on the maintenance of internal processes.

Amdahl manufactures its range of mainframe computers at two sites, one in Sunnyvale, California, and the other at Swords near Dublin in Ireland. Each site manufactures an identical product range using identical processes. They service primarily the North American and European markets from the site that is closest. When one site is unable to supply in the lead time demanded, then the orders are switched to the other. There is no competition between sites for new product, and each has representatives on the EMI teams.

INFORMATION IS THE KEY TO GLOBAL MANUFACTURING

Global manufacturing cannot be achieved unless the operations of the business are totally integrated. Such a level of integration relies heavily on global information networks. With such networks and a common way of working, assets can be managed on a worldwide basis.

Ways of working in global manufacturers place significant demands on managers and include such requirements as providing real-time updates to systems so that the product value chain is continuously visible to staff around the world.

MEASURING LARGE BUSINESSES

In a company operating on a global scale, management accounting cannot be confused with measuring the business. The vagaries of transfer pricing and currency fluctuations cannot be allowed to drive the way the business is run. A meaningful performance architecture must be made up of a few key operations metrics that are sensitive to corporate objectives, product groups and regional requirements.

These metrics must be easily administered, have a clear link to corporate strategy, and force continuous improvement, after reengineering of core business processes has been accomplished. And foremost, they must reflect the four paramount metrics of core processes: *cost, quality, lead time,* and *service*.

For instance, at ABB's power transformer business area headquarters in Mannheim, Germany, a monthly report is created. This report compares how each of the 25 manufacturing facilities performs on such parameters as throughput time (lead time), inventories and receivables as a percentage of revenues (cost), and failure rates (quality). The goal of such reporting is not only to enhance competition among managers over whose plant performs better, but to enhance cooperation and coordination among managers in helping one another solve problems they themselves might have had at another time.

ABB's most famous measurement system, however, is Abacus. This system requires each of the company's 1100 business units to report on a standard form to Zurich each month within days of the month end. The consolidated results are available by the middle of the month to all executives.

Although such a task certainly gives the organization great flexibility to respond to changes in market conditions, it can only be contemplated with the aid of advanced information technology.

PRODUCTS AND SERVICES

By focusing on core business processes, large businesses inevitably drive toward standardization of as much of the product as possible. By focusing on *transferability*, *standards*, and *innovation*, they seek to manufacture so as to be able to ship finished products between markets.

Transferability

By focusing on cost, quality, lead time, and service, the point of manufacture becomes relatively inconsequential. A worldwide schedule can be developed that uses each plant in the global network to its optimum capacity according to demand.

For instance, assume the demand from a geographic sector is 1200 units of production from the nearest plant, but this plant has a design capacity of 1000 units. In a multinational environment, local stocks or overtime would temporarily buffer the surge in demand. But neither is an effective use of assets.

In a process-oriented global business, where there are standardized products, the worldwide scheduler (we discuss an expert system we call Asset Manager later in this chapter) can assign the demand surge to alternative sites.

Air freight costs have been declining since the early 1980s, and for many industries logistics costs are not as critical as they used to be. The cost of excess capacity in the form of under-utilized plant, inventory, support personnel, and space is usually considerably higher than the cost of transportation. In some industries, for example FMCG, transport is less important than the manufacturing process and is actually used to manage the capacity of assets. The arrival of a vehicle for loading becomes the replenishment signal for the plant, which is synonymous with real customer demand.

Multinational manufacturing businesses grew by servicing a number of customer bases in defined market regions. Each site had to forecast demand and build buffer stock in times when demand did not meet forecast. But in today's world, with faster and cheaper transportation, as well as economic alliances such as the European Community, there is far less justification for local manufacturing sites to buffer their own demand.

Because common processes have been transferred between manufacturing sites, customers can now be served from any manufacturing site in the world. Rather than central head-quarters deciding how many units of a product each plant must manufacture, customer demand determines the amount and does it without straining any plant's capacity or creating problems with resources.

Semiconductor manufacturing is now a global manufac-turing business. Front-end plants prepare the die, which can each contain up to 2500 silicon devices. These die are then sent to back-end plants for assembly into components. Back-end plants are normally established in developing nations because of cheap labor and the high labor content in these assembly activities. SGS-Thomson, for example, has such plants in Morocco, Malta, Singapore, and Malaysia. Transportation between front-end and back-end plants, and between back-end plants and the customer is entirely by air. Demand can there-fore be moved to available capacity—which may be on the other side of the world—in a matter of hours.

It is interesting to note that Anchorage, Alaska, has emerged as a major transfer and intermittent stocking point for many industries. This is because an airplane can reach almost any point in the Northern Hemisphere within eight hours from Anchorage.

Standards

Global manufacturing businesses are particularly aware of the trade-offs involved in dealing with technical and other stan-dards. In general, they aim to design so as to reduce the total number of variables that will be encountered. The products, and with them their manufacturing processes, should meet the highest technical, environmental, health, safety, and other standards of all the markets in which they will be sold.

Many companies have previously designed separate products for each national standard, such as an electrical standard in different countries. Today, an increasing number of companies are moving toward common designs for the entire product, except for the actual electrical connector.

The only different part of the CRT manufactured at the three IBM plants discussed above that used EMI teams were the plug and the transformer. These three plants could carry minimal inventory and request support from any other IBM CRT plant in the world should they have difficulties.

In Europe, each country has a different standard plug and Italy even has three. Despite this diversity, NCR's German facility makes all of its product for Europe, and, if necessary, for North America, with the ability to handle any voltage and cycle; a bar code on each unit tells the assembler of plugs which plug to splice on to the cord.

Innovation

In a company operating globally, innovation can occur anywhere. In the old way, innovation is a local issue, and innovations often are not transferred. But in the new way, innovation groups similar to EMI teams work on innovation surrounding a product or product line, with a centrally planned roll out. For process innovations, the local organization implements and then, because of enhanced communication, the innovation moves from location to location.

Done well, empowering innovation groups to explore innovation and manage global rollout while centralizing much of the actual development can lead to high degrees of innovation without sacrificing standardization. Indeed, standardization promotes or enhances innovation, since there are fewer problems to work around and to divert attention from continuous improvement of the process. The team has created a degree of acceptance such that local cultures will often suppress some of their natural "not invented here" thinking.

LOCATING ACTIVITIES

In the company manufacturing globally, while products are able to be shipped between sites throughout the world due to standardization of platforms and uniform quality, the manufacturing processes themselves are centrally managed.

The central responsibilities within a global organization include developing and disseminating corporate objectives throughout the business. Well-articulated statements of "strategic intent" and specific corporate objectives are critical to the success of a global manufacturing organization.

While centralized management of capacity is important, for a global company to be a global local business, there also must be a strong dose of decentralization. This is especially the case in such areas as market management and the identification of local market preferences. While any local business can specify a new product, its design and process roll out should be done centrally, with the business's local objectives accommodated by the EMI team.

Products designed in this way become simultaneously feature rich and customer specific. That is, they offer a broad range of capability in a small number of product variants without appearing to offer features that the customer does not require. For example, Mars Electronics has developed a coin-recognition system that will take any European coin. The different physical characteristics of European coins have been recorded and are stored as data by the software of the recognition device. Thus a British customer, for example, is never aware that he has bought a coin-recognition device that can accept all European coins. He believes that it has been specifically designed for him and only recognizes British coins. The importance of this approach in concealing non-required product features from customers can be readily appreciated. Just how much do non-smokers resent paying for ashtrays in their automobiles?

INFORMATION TECHNOLOGY AS AN ENABLER

The function of daily scheduling of capacity in a global business is too enormous for an individual, or even a centralized department. It is possible to create a fully integrated hardware and software system to enable capacity to be balanced around the world.

This system, which we call the Asset Manager, is likely to use artificial intelligence. The system functions by accepting worldwide orders, reviewing the condition of each manufacturing site and establishing the best possible final assembly schedule for each plant. It then downloads the schedule to each manufacturing site. Figure 7.4 shows some of the parameters the Asset Manager is constantly reviewing.

The Asset Manager provides a mechanism for accepting and scheduling every order every day for manufacture the same day or the next. By reducing planning and manufacturing lead times to a minimum, the point of manufacture becomes relatively inconsequential. The Asset Manager is "free" to schedule each plant in the worldwide network to optimum capacity according to demand.

The Asset Manager as we conceive it requires a set of key information data bases. These data bases include manufacturing and design specifications and quality requirements,

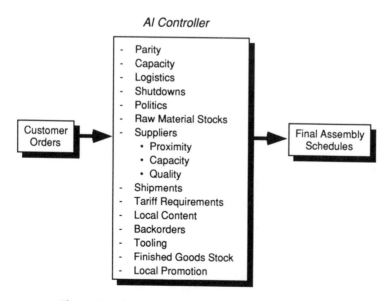

Figure 7.4 *Parameters reviewed by Asset Manager.*

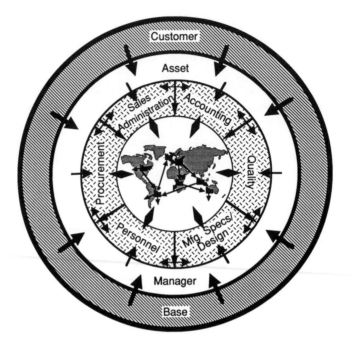

Figure 7.5 *Asset Manager's power and authority in global manufacturing sites.*

procedures, and results. Some of the data would be updated in real time from other centralized data bases, while other data, such as shipments or local promotions, would be updated locally.

The Asset Manager in its own right would provide data to the accounting and control functions. It is a vital tool for sales administrators. The data from the Asset Manager would be used to assess material procurement requirements in the short term and in the long term to give warnings of personnel shortages. Such systems have been created in global businesses today such as Hewlett-Packard, IBM, and Philips; they are the unsung conductors of the global orchestra.

As shown in Figure 7.5, the Asset Manager provides the power and authority for the global manufacturing sites to meet customer demand.

DUPLICATING ACTIVITIES

Global manufacturing businesses do not seek to create duplicate facilities because they have developed the ability to manage them. The economics of scale production still hold true in global businesses. They will set up new operations facilities only when it is absolutely necessary. There are occasions where some characteristic of the process, or access to resources or markets, will dictate that duplicating an activity is the way to proceed.

For example, a core business process in one food processing company is the delivery of pizza to its supermarket customers. It determined that it could achieve a BreakPoint if it could get the freshest pizzas into the stores. Because of new process and packaging technology, the business knew in 1989 that it would be possible to produce pizza for the chilled (refrigerated) section of U.K. supermarkets rather than as a frozen food. It needed to decide how to proceed. Since the process of making a pizza to freeze and one to deliver "fresh" to the chilled-food supermarket aisle is different, the company needed a new production facility.

It was possible to build a new plant in Ireland to expand the existing facilities, or to acquire a competitor with U.K. manufacturing facilities, to manufacture the pizza. The decision was eventually made to build a new plant in Ireland because of the good transport facilities, the low cost of capital, and the favorable tax regime. This was despite the apparent difficulties of transporting chilled pizza over the sea.

A further reason for duplicating operations in a particular country is because of that country's regulations with regard to local content or offset. For instance, many nationalized businesses will only purchase from local subcontractors. But when quality and dimensions are standardized on a worldwide basis, one plant can make and transship to another country if need be.

Because of the way it has grown by acquisition, ABB has the best of both worlds. In products where local content is not an issue and standardization is fairly easy to accomplish, ABB has been able to rationalize operations and pare manufacturing capacity. But in areas where local content is an issue, ABB's advantage lies in its system of local business entities—many of which existed in their place of origin before ABB came on to the scene—rather than just distribution and marketing relationships. In this way it has an ability to claim a legitimate local presence and thus to sell its equipment to government entities.

This chapter has focused on the special opportunities and difficulties of large businesses when trying to employ a process orientation. As businesses inevitably grow and move toward being global they have an opportunity to dominate their markets. But such domination will not come from merely employing economies of scale; rather it will come from a rigorous process orientation and focus on customer value.

Such an orientation implies that new supporting processes must be created, including EMI teams, and possibly expert-system asset management systems for the new assets. In order to create products and services that provide superior value to customers, large companies must also engage in two new activities: they must understand what gives customer value and they must personally engage in the reengineering of their core business processes.

8
Organizing and Managing for Success

Because Business Process Reengineering seeks to make radical changes in the way a business operates, it is necessary to make concomitant changes in the business as an organic entity. In order to do this, management needs to use a number of tools and techniques that have been emerging since the early 1980s under the umbrella of "change management."

The areas within a business that need to be changed include culture, structure, performance measurement, incentive systems, and management style.

Culture is the most difficult to change, since it ultimately involves the behavior of all employees as the company migrates from one that can be described as command and control of functions to a delayered environment that emphasizes process excellence through teamwork.

Structure in the new organization must accommodate a balance between functional expertise and process involvement. A structure that has removed functional barriers to accommodate the mobility of team members in and out of process reengineering and improvement roles is essential.

Performance measurement will focus on the team and team members' contribution to enhanced competitiveness through improvements in cost, quality, time, and service as they relate to core business processes. Contribution will be acknowledged by various forms of company recognition linked directly to achievements in core process improvement. Incentive systems that focus on the individual will first be deemphasized, then disappear completely.

Management will champion the change, emphasizing shared values and a vision of excellence through empowerment of all members of the workforce and investment to enable continuous process improvement.

The overall approach to successful change management has become understood in the last few years. The general framework used in Business Process Reengineering is in line with the latest thinking on change management.

It is not the purpose of this book to be prescriptive about change management; there is a large body of literature in that regard. In this chapter, rather, we will be descriptive about five aspects of the organization as it goes from being functionally oriented to process oriented, and how it will operate in a process oriented environment. These five aspects are:

1 the leader;
2 the business unit leader;
3 the new organization;
4 the transition organization that will lead from the old way to the new way, from functional orientation to process orientation;
5 the individual within the new organization.

THE LEADER

The tools and techniques of change management lack credibility except in the hands of certain individuals who by force of character and leadership are able to create and sustain a vision that is meaningful to employees. Attempts to codify the mechanisms of change management have failed; while experts can show why a particular change effort succeeded where others failed, they are unable to predict the detailed approach that should be adopted in any new situation.

The business leaders and senior managers interviewed for this book seem to possess many of the characteristics and qualities of Olympic athletes. The successful leader in a process-oriented company is continually drawing himself and those who report to him to "personal best" achievement. Both the athlete and the business leader see personal performance as the primary driver and the managing of a company or the athletic event as a secondary goal.

The CEOs who have succeeded in breaking their business away from traditional functional perspectives and in introducing a process orientation are those who have worked out what their personal best performance should be, and how to act in order to deliver it day after day.

An example of this dedication is Percy Barnevik, the CEO of ABB, who sets himself the target of visiting as many of his 1100 businesses as possible each year. He prides himself that he will reply to any message that arrives in his office for his attention within 24 hours.

Larry Bossidy of Allied-Signal was a star baseball pitcher, and today carries that same drive to make Allied-Signal the best. Eldon Auker, a World Series winning pitcher, took tiny Bay State Abrasives to a position of number two in the world in its market. Roger Penske used the same drive to develop a multi-billion dollar group of industries that he did to win the Indianapolis 500 automobile race; he was at one time a leading candidate for the chairmanship of General Motors.

All of these leaders drove themselves to excellence, and that characteristic was infectious to their subordinates. In short, the leader of a large company that is striving toward process excellence has a vision coupled with values that include customer focus, doing right by suppliers and employees as well as shareholders, and the desire for all in the organization to strive for personal-best performance.

These leaders openly display personal behaviour that models both the vision and the values, setting an example for others in the organization, especially the business unit leaders who will have to do the nuts-and-bolts work of determining the core business processes in their business unit and leading the business unit through the Business Process Reengineering undertaking.

A key capability of superior leaders is the ability to communicate the vision and values to business unit leaders and corporate employees; and the security in one's own ego to allow business unit leaders to grasp the vision and refine it so that it can be acted upon at the business unit level. However, grasping and refining the vision must assume a sense of urgency and inescapability for business unit leaders. Bossidy of Allied-Signal tells his top business unit managers that they will move toward process orientation or they will go home and work on their résumés (CVs).

Realization of the vision requires a goal-setting process that drives the organization in lock-step toward process excellence. Bossidy of Allied-Signal has adopted "Total Quality Through Speed" as a central theme.

The TQS umbrella provides a common language throughout the organization that is established from company-wide training in the management approach and the tools and techniques for cycle-time reduction applied to all company processes. TQS communicates a simple and straight message to all employees, a message that emphasizes a strong focus on process, customers, and anticipation of change.

In this way, it is clear to all that productivity is a way of life, and that continuous quality, cost, time, and service improvements in core business processes will remain at the top of his agenda. Bossidy enables continuous improvement through broad-scale investment in people, and by instituting "best practices" throughout the corporation through communication among business unit leaders. Allied-Signal's commitment to train 50 000 employees in TQS in a single year stands as Bossidy's clear message to his organization regarding his commitment to realize his vision of process excellence.

Fear of failure, fueled by a management style that punishes mistakes rather than using them as an opportunity for improvement, leads to hiding poor performance and inhibits people from any risk taking. Leaders of process-oriented companies allow business unit leaders to challenge the assumptions and principles on which the business is currently run, understanding that mistakes will be made, but that through these mistakes will come a richer understanding of the processes on which to focus.

The goal of leadership both at the corporate and business unit level in Business Process Reengineering is to move from a more autocratic style to a more coaching style, creating vision that others can understand and accept. These leaders constantly refocus their business on the customer, insist on processes that will provide the products and services that their customers will value above those of the competition and, finally, manage the new assets that are required by the processes.

The level of dedication to personal best performance in everything they do does not remain at the top of an organization. A new vocabulary has been introduced to management teams in the leading companies. Ultimately, the end game is an organization where all individuals are *enabled* and *empowered* through principles of *intrapreneurship* to the point of pursuing innovation and creativity, and being able to work constantly toward BreakPoints.

BUSINESS UNIT LEADER

The business unit leader is the person who drives the Business Process Reengineering undertaking, which involves both organizing the business activities and managing the change process.

Because he or she has profit and loss responsibility, the business unit leader must weigh the magnitude and speed of change against the day-to-day operation of the business in the "as-is" state. The business unit leader asks the questions:

- What business am I in, and do my core business processes provide the capability needed for market leadership?
- Who are my customers, and how can I use core business processes to deliver superior value?
- What will my business unit look like if we push our processes to their ultimate level of performance?
- What core business processes in my business enable me and the corporate leader to reach our visions, both for the larger organization and for my business unit?

The business unit leader sets performance goals and measures for the business, develops the plan, finds the best and brightest people to head the Business Process Reengineering undertaking, and provides the time, money and "empowerment" necessary for the undertaking to go forward.

A superior business unit leader has the ability to take the macro-level vision developed by the corporate leader and translate it into an operational vision and plan for his or her business unit. This leader must also have a high tolerance for working amidst chaos—when one breaks the china there is a period of vast upheaval while a new way of operating is instituted. This leader also needs to have the ability to work not only across functional boundaries but also across corporate boundaries, for he or she will spearhead any attempts to create virtual core business processes that cross corporate lines.

A business unit leader needs to encourage and motivate the workforce to grasp the vision, and must constantly champion the undertaking. Not only that, a business unit leader must be sensitive to the need to roll out his vision for the business in steps, as a series of short-term goals.

As Andy Guarriello of AT&T Power Systems said, by 1989 he had the basic vision for 1995, but by 1992 he had only articulated about 50 percent to his workforce. Had he let too much of the vision out too early, he fears, he would have frightened his employees into a state of paralysis.

Although the tone is set at the corporate level, it is at the business unit level that real changes occur in the corporate culture. This is true since different business units often have their own cultures, and because the business unit is where leadership really gets a chance to do hands-on management. The business unit level is where the action is; where the core business processes are defined, and where cross-functional, multidimensional teams are formed. Importantly, the business unit level is where most of the human resource professionals within a business are most often located.

Change management requires a clear understanding of the existing culture and behavior patterns of the people in a business, and a deliberate attempt to change this into some other form of behavior.

Culture is usually defined as "the commonly held values and attitudes that determine behavior," or "the way we do things around here." Whatever the definition, organizational culture is a powerful determinant of how everyone behaves in an organization. The stronger the behavioral norms, the more consistent and coordinated behavior becomes. There is evidence from organizations in both the East and the West that organizations with well-understood norms of behavior produce focused, high performing employees.

Within a corporate culture are the company's values. While Business Process Reengineering does not connote a specific set of values, the goals of BPR (breaking down functional barriers and thinking of business activities as processes) do force many companies to modify their values.

THE NEW ORGANIZATION

The new organization will have a drastically different look than the old organization. Work will be done in process teams, supported by small cadres of functional specialists. The hierarchy will be flattened. The focus will be external—on the customer and the supplier, with whom the company has entered into partnership—rather than internal, with all of its questions about who fits where on the organizational chart.

Teams will be "self managing" in that they will not have layers of supervisors and managers overseeing them. But they will not create and direct their own efforts; rather they will understand the role they are to play in the overall effectiveness of the process.

Their tasks will be assigned, during the transition period by the steering committee or the program management committee, and after the organization is process oriented by the leadership. Teams will be measured on the four metrics of *cost, quality, time* and *service*.

Perhaps the most important value that BPR either forces or reinforces is teamwork. The creation and deployment of multi-faceted, cross-functional teams is perhaps the most important enabler of Business Process Reengineering. The performance of teams has been consistently shown to be better than individuals on almost any task, no matter how dedicated or talented the individual involved.

Hierarchical, bureaucratic organizations leave people feeling powerless. In Europe and the United States, there has been since the late 1980s a move away from hierarchical to team-based structures as part of a trend toward developing more responsive and flexible organizations. The Japanese, of course, have run team-based organizations for many years.

Western companies find the change to a team-based organization difficult because their systems, processes, and practices tend to focus on individual effort and top–down control within a functional context.

In most Western businesses, departmental processes are much stronger than business processes. Attempts to integrate departments and improve customer service are often thwarted by departmental managers who see only that they will lose power through integration. In order for teams to be truly effective, people coming into the team from different functions must learn to trust one another. One of the key jobs of business unit leaders is to build and foster that trust, to reward trust, and to force those who cannot learn to trust and be a part of the team to leave.

In the new organization, restructuring will not be an occasional occurrence, usually taking place around a change in leadership or a need to correct poor performance. Rather, restructuring will be constant, with teams disbanding and new teams forming in order to face effectively myriad new challenges. If the old organization was a machine, the new organization is a living organism, constantly adapting.

While many companies say they value teamwork, they actually reward individual compliance with orders from above. These conflicting messages result in cynicism and distrust of management motives when restructuring is implemented.

Both financial reward and various kinds of recognition—showing appreciation—are team based. Frequent recognition for seemingly small yet important efforts is often used. In the area of changing rewards, gainsharing and pay-for-knowlege are becoming more common.

The process orientation will grow in the new organization as the company realizes enhanced competitiveness and creation of value for customers. As benefits accrue, process reengineering and improvement efforts will move to a broad scale encompassing all core business processes in the company.

The greater emphasis on the team, knowledge, and process improvement contribution as the basis for reward and recognition are natural consequences of this movement.

Career paths will take on new dimensions, reaching a point where process leadership gains in stature and equals, then surpasses, functional leadership as the path toward increased management responsibility. When the movement reaches "steady state" functions and process champions will co-exist, but the individuals running the business will be the process leaders.

THE TRANSITION ORGANIZATION

Managing the transition period between the organization's functional state and its process-oriented state is no easy task. Although it is easy to recognize what should be done, and what the organization will look like after processes become the main organizing theme—and it is especially easy for a business unit manager to nod his or her head when the corporate leader says "you will become process oriented or you will rewrite your résumé"—conducting the transition is somewhat akin to tightrope walking without a net.

It can be made easier by thinking of the transition itself as a process, a cascading process that might be seen in one of a few ways:

- As the tide comes in at the seashore, a sandcastle that has been built (the functional, hierarchical organization) is slowly eroded. At the same time, a new, parallel sandcastle (the process organization) is being built above the high-tide line.
- The hero of the latest computer game (process man) moves across the screen gobbling bits of the functional empire, until he has devoured the functional organization.

However one chooses to look at this metamorphosis, the important thing to remember is that *there is a structure during the Business Process Reengineering undertaking.* That structure involves:

- the business unit leader;
- the steering committee;
- the program management committee;

- the design team.
- task teams;

The business unit leader essentially chooses those who will sit on the steering committee, then gets out of the way, focusing his energy on running the day-to-day operations, while at the same time championing the change to a process orientation. He tries not to give conflicting signals between what he says and the management decisions he makes. It takes a finely tuned ego, one that doesn't mind being, in essence, a lame duck leader, knowing that one day when the transformation is complete one's leadership role will be completely different than it used to be (although many of the best business unit leaders exhibit process- and team-oriented qualities far before the formal change occurs).

The steering committee is responsible for choosing the order in which the core processes are to be redesigned. It sets goals, puts task teams together to perform the redesign, draws up plans for the redesign effort, and monitors results against the plan.

The steering committee sets the priorities for process redesign in order to achieve some early successes to assure continued high morale in the effort.

Task teams are very specifically assigned tasks by the steering committee. Most focus on one core business process that is being redesigned. But others have tasks that cut across processes; for instance, one task team will be charged with focusing on organizational culture changes, one with designing new individual performance appraisal material, etc.

The program management committee is, in essence, the middle management of the transition. It interacts with the task teams, coaching them, lobbying the steering committee on their behalf, and making sure that the Business Process Reengineering effort is not interfering with the day-to-day operation of the business.

The design team exists for a short period at the beginning of the undertaking. It literally "designs the future," doing the nitty-gritty analysis work described in Chapter 4. In some instances the design team may become the program management team. But in other instances, especially when the amount of analysis is great, or the analysis of some operations needs to be performed well after the first processes are being redesigned, the two groups will be separate, and when the design team's work is over it will simply fold up.

In some ways, the transition organization is an overlay over the functional organization. Although it is cumbersome—and in some ways counter to its own goals of delayering and defunctionalizing—it assures continuity during the transition. Most task teams are dismantled as their task is completed, and as more and more task teams are dismantled, the bureaucracy of the transition organization lessens. Eventually, like the cocoon in which the caterpillar metamorphoses into the butterfly, the transition organization structure comes apart.

This overlay does not mean extra bodies. Instead, it is a redeployment of people from function to transition to process. The balance of how many people are working functionally, within the transition, and in a process orientation, is what changes over time.

The entire transition effort is a very delicate undertaking. It requires close coordination between the business unit leader, the steering and program management committees, and the corporate leader. If not handled with extreme care, the entire effort can collapse.

Throughout the transition period, there is a need to change management practices. To do this, early involvement of managers at all levels is important, because the greatest resistance to changes comes from them. They fear loss of power from change, and as a result they often quietly yet efficiently block change initiatives.

Managers will only feel a sense of ownership if they are allowed to help establish the measures of success—how success is defined and measured. They should measure everything they can, so that the change effort does not become vague or lose momentum.

Once managers know what changes have to take place and how they will happen—and their role in those changes—they will start to influence behavior of staff, focus on results, and release their creative talent. They also start changing their roles, becoming less concerned with control and instruction, and more concerned with challenge and discussion. With this change of management style, organizational politics can be cast aside to allow for free-wheeling discussion and more creative management.

Managing change this way carries risks for a CEO (both the business unit leader and the corporate leader) and the senior executive team, because they lose day-to-day control of the change effort. But they need to take that step, because the only successful way to change management practice—and ultimately corporate culture—is for a critical mass of managers to become committed to the effort and drive it deep into the fiber of the company.

INDIVIDUALS

Individuals in the process-oriented organization will be able to work comfortably in teams because they will have been given the right tools to function that way. They will have broadened skills, including analytical and interpersonal skills, a commonality of language across the organization, an appreciation of each other's needs, and a better understanding of how things fit together. They will be linked by common values, and be highly motivated.

Gaining these tools, experiences, and abilities will not only be their responsibility. It will be the responsibility of the process-oriented organization and its leadership. Once given the opportunity to gain these tools, experiences, and abilities, it will be up to individual employees either to avail themselves of the opportunity and stay with the company, or to find another place to work that does not put as much responsibility on them.

There will be two main ways of getting people to continue upgrading their skills. One is peer pressure to do things the right way, to keep up, and to contribute to the effort of the team, the business unit, and ultimately the company.

In the company that functions as a living organism, continuous learning is imperative. Innovation and risk taking are essential elements in such an organization. For innovation and risk taking to be nurtured, a learning atmosphere needs to be developed in which experiences, whether successful or not, are rapidly assimilated and form the basis of learning how to cope with change.

When individuals are encouraged to learn, regardless of the immediate payback to the company in terms of productivity improvement, they begin to think differently. They challenge; they look for answers to complex problems. In the long run, the rewards to the company for encouraging learning far outweigh the initial costs.

Continuous learning will soon be an integral part of every manager's job. For this learning to be effective, it must be integrated into the career path of the individual, and it must be accepted as part of the problem-solving process followed by the company in its transition from current to desired state.

The training itself should be wide ranging to provide learning on thinking and feeling levels, and be firmly geared to helping everyone in the company involved in the change process to appreciate the impact of what they are doing.

Only by taking learning seriously on both the organizational and individual levels can a company functioning as a living organism nurture and renew itself. If learning is not taken seriously, then only the bureaucratic, hierarchical model of organization is workable, in which effort is focused on routine and ritual, and which presupposes that no change is necessary.

The other area that will change drastically with regard to individuals is the reward and incentive system. In the process-oriented company, people are paid according to their contribution and their effort, not by their seniority and not necessarily by their position in the hierarchy. People are, in effect, "paid for their toolbox." As individuals become more skilled at more tasks, able to shift from one piece of the process to another and contribute to more different task teams, they are paid more. In addition, recognition gets more closely tied to rewards, and recognition becomes team rather than individual oriented.

No longer do individuals see their career as a 'ladder,' but rather as a series of steps that look lateral on an organizational chart, but that constitute movement to new, different, and more challenging opportunities, and often to leadership of larger and more complex teams.

For many, this is difficult to accept. But in the organizations within which it has been tried and successfully put in place, many more have increased their morale, their productivity, and most important, their creativity.

As Larry Bossidy, the CEO of Allied-Signal, said, "Good people beget good people. Well-managed marginal players become good players far more often than not. At the end of the day, a lot of measurements remain financial. But a lot of other things will need to be measured in the future. *Good numbers are a result of good things happening* [our italics]."

9
A Final Word

As each day goes by and we get closer and closer to the twenty-first century, it is increasingly apparent that the survivors in this new era of business will be those companies that are rigorous in their pursuit of three concurrent goals: customer satisfaction, market domination, and increased profitability. One without the other two is clearly not sufficient for a winning business in the new era.

It is also increasingly clear that the only way to pursue these three goals simultaneously is for a company continually to define itself, by the business it is in, the market it seeks to control, the customers it seeks to attract, and most importantly by the core business processes that drive it.

It will be up to those who read this book to act on its suggestions, putting the ideas laid out here into the context of their own business environment.

It will be up to corporate leaders to create a vision: of competitive dominance rather than mere parity; of teamwork and team reward rather than internal competition for coveted individual honours—businesses run on what Larry Bossidy of Allied-Signal calls his three tenets of "customers, productivity, and involvement of all people"; of business unit decisions being made in the manner Percy Barnevik of Asea Brown Boveri describes as: "fast, fact-driven, and with no favoritism."

It will be up to business unit leaders to take that corporate vision and translate it into an operational vision for his or her business, people, products, customers, and suppliers. This can only be done by constantly asking the most profound question a business leader can ask: Why?

- Why are we in the business we are in?
- Why do we operate the way we do?
- Why do we need. . . in order to fulfill our mission?
- Why. . .?
- Why. . .?

Only by torturing himself and those who report directly to him by constantly asking "why?" can a business unit leader determine the three or four core business processes that encompass the true competitive dimensions and key competencies of the business unit. And only by focusing the business unit's energy on reengineering those core business processes to enrich them—to turbocharge them—can the business unit leader drive the business unit to the heights of competitive excellence and ultimately to marketplace domination.

As has been said, few business unit leaders set out to find a BreakPoint by design; rather, what they do is embark on a quest they believe will be never ending, to find the pot of gold at the end of the rainbow. Along the way, by concentrating on the core business processes, they find ways to bring their business unit to the point of best in class; they find other ways to get their business unit ahead of the competition in one or more of the competitive dimensions in their industry.

If they work hard enough, listen to those within the business unit who have good ideas, have a little luck, and are willing to take a few hits (and have a corporate management willing to let them take some hits) they may even find the BreakPoint, the key competitive dimension that causes the marketplace to say "WOW."

Regardless of whether a Breakpoint is achieved, however, Business Process Reengineering is a powerful tool of modern management. It forces leaders at both the corporate and business unit level to rethink the organizing principles on which their business is built and run. It gets them away from the old formulation of cost or profit; by thinking of process enhancement, one can see how the pieces of a business's operations fit together, and how by planing the corners of the various activities so they fit together more tightly, business operations become not only more efficient but more effective, cost naturally declines, and profits are enhanced.

In order to identify successfully core business processes, and subsequently reengineer them, business leaders need to focus on the "new assets," such as human talent, proprietary intellectual property, brands, and information, rather than merely focusing on the old assets of cash and property. If the new assets are properly managed, and core business processes successfully reengineered, the new assets will manage the old assets, creating continued corporate wealth and health.

But, as the old adage goes, "you have to spend money to make money." Business Process Reengineering is not a panacea, and it is certainly not without costs: monetary, emotional, organizational, and in terms of time. A process orientation is a whole new way of looking at the way a business works, and as such the costs of organizing, planning, training, and ramping up into a process-oriented business are not insignificant. These costs must be accepted by corporate leadership at the outset, and articulated to investors.

Frequently throughout the Business Process Reengineering undertaking—which is measured in time in terms of years rather than months or weeks—corporate leadership must sit back, take stock and reaffirm its commitment. If the commitment slips, and the old ways of measuring results, rewarding, and creating incentives, come back in while those in the trenches at the business unit level are working toward process orientation, those people will feel they have had their efforts cut out from under them.

In short, finding core business processes and engaging in Business Process Reengineering is not easy, but it is vitally important if Western companies are to continue being competitive in an increasingly global world.

And only those who read and lead will be able to make such Business Process Reengineering efforts successful.

Appendix
Process Mapping

An indispensable tool in Business Process Reengineering is process mapping. Competitive realignment through identifying and exploiting BreakPoints is achieved by reengineering core business processes. This, in turn, requires an extensive understanding of the activities that constitute core business processes and the processes that support them, in terms of their purpose, trigger points, inputs and outputs and constraining influences. This understanding can better be achieved by "mapping," "modeling" and then measuring the processes using various techniques that have been developed and refined over the years. In this Appendix further insight is given in the use of these techniques and their normal domains of application.

DEFINITION OF A PROCESS

"A process is a set of linked activities that take an input and transform it to create an output."

We may refer to stages in a process as subprocesses when the activities that constitute the subprocess are so complex as to warrant such treatment or in cases where the process itself is more easily understood by a decomposition "top-down." Processes can be physical, involve paperwork, be undertaken by computer, or be a logical sequence of events, as shown in the various examples in Figure A.1.

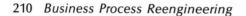

• Physical

e.g. Materials Supply Chain

• On Paper

e.g. Bid Preparation

• Logical

e.g. Order Entry, Procurement

The product development process ...

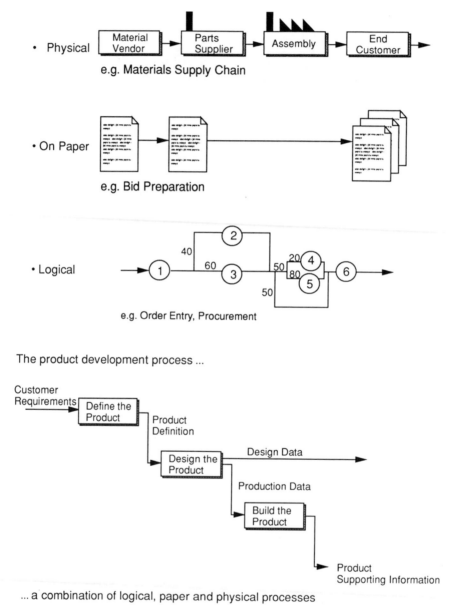

... a combination of logical, paper and physical processes

Figure A.1   *About processes.*

In many cases the four types of process shown schematically in Figure A.1 exist together as, for example, with the logical sequencing of activities required to start up or shut down a chemical process. In the same way in a business process such as satisfying customer orders, order documentation usually precedes a process to manufacture items.

DATA MODELING

Process mapping can be supplemented by a technique called data modeling. Data modeling evolved from a growing recognition of the need to manage data as an asset. The two techniques should not be confused; data modeling is not a substitute for process mapping. In data modeling, the aim is to understand the relationships between data elements and the links between the data sets in which the data elements may be present. In this way efficiencies are sought in the capture, ownership and dissemination of data, to avoid unnecessary duplication and overlap, and to maintain the value of the data as an asset.

Process mapping seeks to understand existing and possible future business processes in order to create enhanced customer satisfaction and improved business performance. In processes that depend heavily on the existence of complex and widely distributed data, for example an airline booking system, data modeling is needed in support of process mapping in order to create radically new business processes with a critical dependence on state-of-the-art data management.

ORIGINS OF PROCESS MAPPING

Process mapping has its roots in a variety of areas:

- Work study in factories, in which industrial engineers seek, using scientific methods of observation, data collection and analysis, to make work more productive.
- Organization and method studies, in which office operations are analysed to achieve even loading and efficient utilization of clerical time.
- Process control, in which the dynamic characteristics of production facilities are analyzed as a basis for gathering

information and then using this data to control outputs by adjusting inputs to the process.

- Process simulation, in which complex processes such as nuclear reactors, chemical plants or highly automated facilities in the engineering industry are modeled on computers or by other means to test their response to a wide variety of operating conditions.
- Business modeling, in which, as an aid to corporate planning, business results are predicted in a simulation using mathematical and statistical modeling techniques in order to gain an understanding of the impact of major influences such as price, volume, capacity and input costs.
- Systems engineering and analysis, in which flow diagrams are used to define the operation of procedures for which the intention is to utilize computers and telecommunications equipment to affect some or all of the process.

It may fairly be said that the origin of most of these techniques can be attributed to the American, F. W. Taylor, who began his studies into better methods of doing work in the Midvale Steel Works in the 1880s. Although man has always sought to find easier and better ways of doing things, the original emphasis was more focused on designing equipment or new mechanisms to save work. With the arrival of Taylor it became rewarding to study the way that men—rather than machines—could improve the way work was done. This legacy is with us to this day, although the emphasis in reengineering is to start with the boundaries of a process and look at how all elements—people, machines, organization, and supporting infrastructure—need to be reconfigured to achieve higher levels of performance.

Work Study is defined[1] as a tool or technique of management involving the analytical study of a job or operation for one or both of the following purposes:

- The determination of what exactly has to be done; the optimum conditions—methods, layout, batch size, and equipment; and what causes of ineffective work can be removed.

---

[1] The definition of Work Study is taken from *The Principles and Practice of Management*, edited by E. F. L. Brech, 2nd edn, Longman.

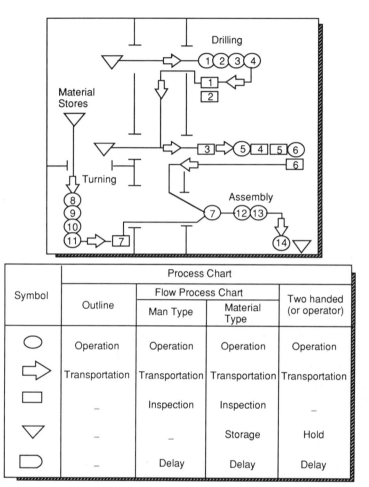

Symbol	Process Chart			
	Outline	Flow Process Chart		Two handed (or operator)
		Man Type	Material Type	
◯	Operation	Operation	Operation	Operation
⇨	Transportation	Transportation	Transportation	Transportation
▭	–	Inspection	Inspection	–
▽	–	–	Storage	Hold
▱	–	Delay	Delay	Delay

Operation - indicates the main steps in a process method or procedure. Usually the part, material or product concerned is modified or changed during the operation.

Transportation - indicates the movement of workers, materials or equipment from place to place.

Storage - indicates a controlled storage in which material is received into or issued from store under some form of authorisation, or an item is retained for reference purposes.

Delay - indicates a delay in the sequence of events, for example work waiting between consecutive operations, or any object laid aside temporarily without record until required.

Inspection - indicates an inspection for quality and/or check for quantity.

Hold - indicates the retention of an object in one hand, normally so that the other hand may do something to it.

Figure A.2 *A Flow Diagram.*

- The measurement of the work content of the job for use in planning, costing, wage payment (incentive), and control.

The aims of Work Study are to establish the most efficient way of doing the work, standardize on this method, establish the time required, and then install the work method as standard practice. Techniques that have evolved from work study include:

Flow Diagram: a scale diagram showing the location of specific activities and the sequences of men/machines/materials/ equipment used in a process.

String Diagram: a scale plan showing the movement of men or materials using "string" to follow the paths of each, as in Figure A.3 (very similar to Flow Diagrams).

Travel Chart: a tabular record with data about the movement of the resources used in production.

Photographic Records: a recording of movements on the shop floor using a camera over a fixed period of time; the method has gained in popularity with the advent of low-cost video recording equipment with superimposed elapsed time.

Multiple Activity Charts: these charts summarize a number of activities that take place concurrently in order to represent in schematic form situations in which many activities in a process are taking place in parallel (see Figure A.4).

Process Charts: which map a sequence of events represented by using standard symbols (see Figures A.5 and A.6).

From Taylor's original work on the productivity of lathe operators, other applications were quickly found that created phenomenal advances in productivity. For example, Gilbreth successfully applied time-and-motion study to more than double the output of skilled American bricklayers. As the number of people trained in work study techniques grew, new applications were found. These applications continued to be in the manufacturing area and were applied by industrial engineers looking for higher and higher levels of labor productivity.

Times calculated using the techniques were ideally suited to balancing production lines and identifying idle time, and therefore played an important part in the successful

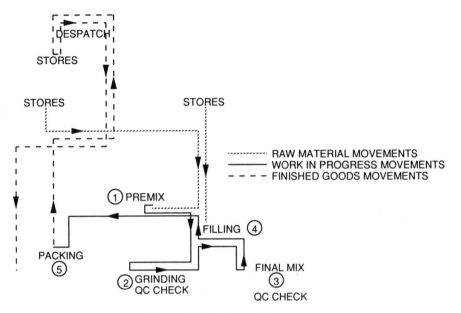

Figure A.3 *A String Diagram.*

adoption of mass-production techniques. As the techniques spread throughout industry and became widely used in the calculation of pay through piecework incentive systems, the work study man, or industrial engineer as he is called in the United States, became one of the most hated men in the Western world as he sought successfully to tighten up the rates and require production operators to work harder and harder for the same money.

The techniques that had found such promising initial application in industry were found to be no less useful in office environments. Multiple Activity Charts were used in a study of work methods in post offices. It had previously been the practice to allocate certain jobs to different counters in the post office. Using work study it was possible to show that working in the traditional manner, loading of the counters was uneven, and that by a reallocation of tasks, a better distribution of work could be achieved. Through this and other examples the techniques spread into the office environment.

216

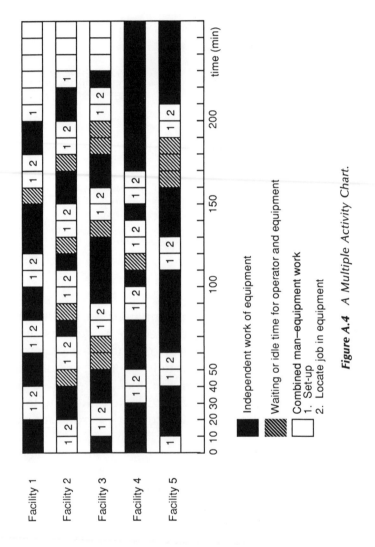

Figure A.4 *A Multiple Activity Chart.*

217

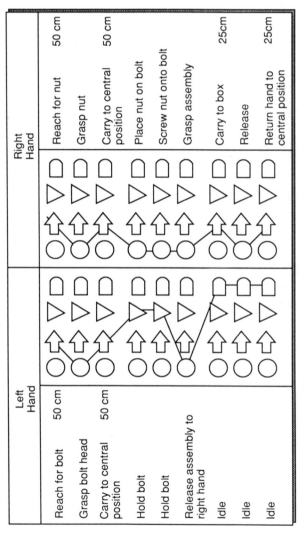

Figure A.5 A two-handed Process Chart.

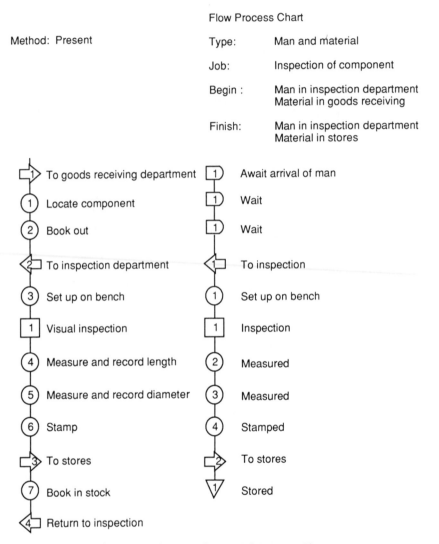

Flow Process Chart

Method: Present

Type: Man and material

Job: Inspection of component

Begin :   Man in inspection department
            Material in goods receiving

Finish: Man in inspection department
            Material in stores

Figure A.6 *Man and material Process Chart.*

COMPUTER FLOWCHARTS

With the arrival of computers onto the business scene, techniques were needed to translate functional requirements into a process suitable for encoding as computer instructions.

Conventions became established for the creation and use of

these flowcharts, and a whole generation of systems analysts became adept at the use of flow charting templates. A typical example of a flowchart created by this means is shown in Figure A.7. In such a flowchart the sequence of work flows from the top to the bottom of the page and standard elements or operations such as data storage, a printed document, undertaking a task, and providing inquiry facilities are represented by standard symbols.

As already mentioned, data flow diagrams made their appearance to document the data relationships inherent in linked activities such as invoicing, pricing, and costing. As the computer technology advanced and databases became an

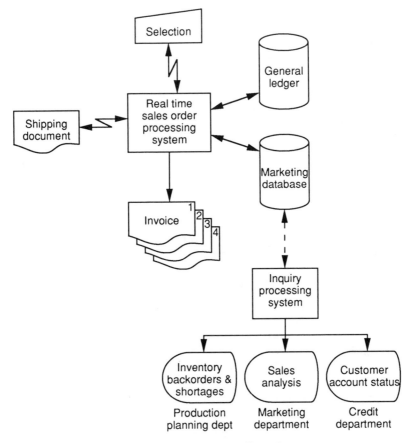

Figure A.7 *A computer flow chart.*

integral part of the business processes, data representation became ever more important. Figure A.8 is an example of a dataflow diagram.

Data-driven process mapping techniques have been found very useful by the authors to support the management of data integration of systems and the building of computer databases.

One such approach was developed by the United States Air

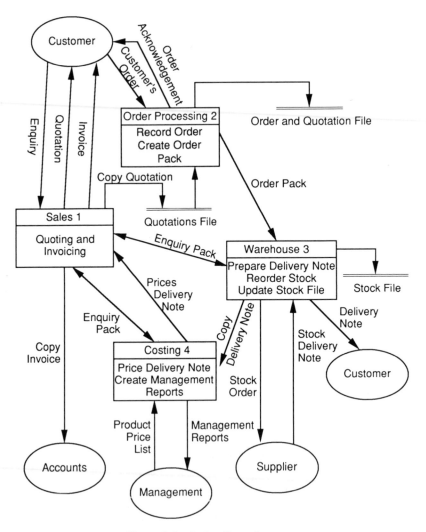

Figure A.8 *A dataflow diagram.*

Force in the mid-1970s. The approach was named International Definition (IDEF), and was instigated under the auspices of the Integrated Computer Aided Manufacturing Program (ICAM), which had identified the need for better analysis and communication techniques for people involved in improving manufacturing productivity.

The approach adopted in IDEF is to describe each process (or activity) as a combination of processes, inputs, controls and mechanisms, as shown in Figure A.9.

At the highest level the representation may be of an entire business process. Next, the process defined at this level of aggregation is broken down into several more activity boxes at one level lower. In such a fashion, the breakdown continues as shown in Figure A.10 until the point is reached where sufficient detail is at hand to make the changes that might be needed.

IDEF offers several advantages to the process analyst:

- The hierarchical structure facilitates "quick mapping" at a high level; very important when looking for radical change.
- By working backwards along the chain from outputs to inputs, much non-value adding work, data, and constraints, can be eliminated.

In view of its origins, IDEF has been particularly heavily used in the aerospace industry, but the same techniques are proving

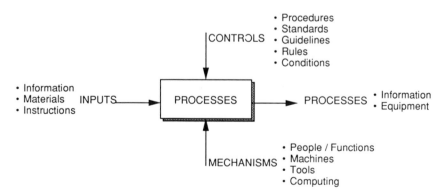

Figure A.9 *The IDEF building block.*

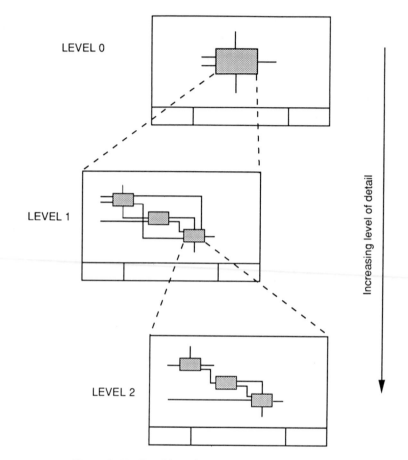

Figure A.10 *Breaking down a process using IDEF.*

useful in sectors such as electronics, pharmaceuticals and fast-moving consumer goods.

An IDEF breakdown of an engineering design and handover process is shown schematically in Figure A.11.

GENERAL BUSINESS MODELING

Business models are useful in understanding the importance of processes in contributing to business performance as in the "road map" diagram shown in Figure A.12. In these

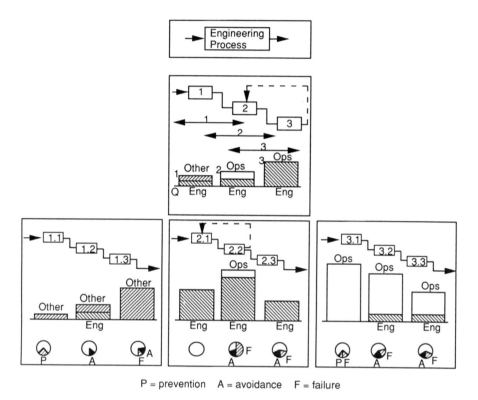

P = prevention   A = avoidance   F = failure

Figure A.11 *A typical use of IDEF.*

representations the objective sought is displayed at the highest level and the contributing subgoals leading to the fulfillment of the objective are then identified as necessary components. In this sense the representation is similar in concept to the Ishikawa or fish bone diagram used to trace problems back to their root causes, and also to the business ratio decomposition methods successfully used by Dupont since the end of the Second World War.

There are, of course, a wide variety of business models in regular use and it is beyond the scope of this Appendix to address all of the possibilities. They include accounting models, stochastic simulators, marketing and pricing models, linear programming models used to optimize production mixes, production modeling, and distribution modeling techniques for warehouse location and vehicle routing.

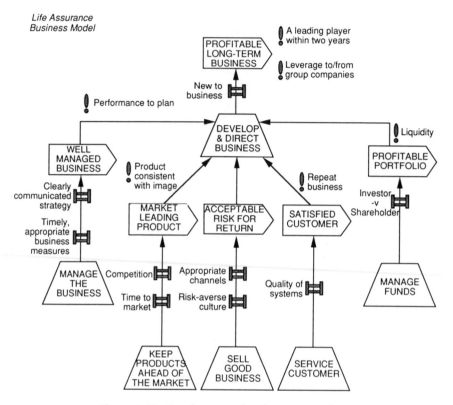

Figure A.12   *Road map style of representation.*

Any of these modeling techniques has potential to aid in Business Process Reengineering, and their use in the appropriate situation has to be decided upon in the fullest knowledge of their capability.

COMPUTER-BASED PROCESS MAPPING

While the variety of analytical tools available to assist the process analyst has developed over a considerable period of time, there has been a parallel but more rapid development in computer-based tools.

Industrial process simulation has advanced enormously over the last 10 years as the power and speed of computers has been applied to progressively greater levels of detail and more broadly scoped simulation exercises. Computer tools are now available to simulate the operation of chemical plants, machine tools, automated logistics systems and complex man–machine interactions. These tools are without doubt an effective means of investigating industrial operations with their capability to simulate successfully, or predict:

- Throughput and costs.
- Operator utilization.
- Machine utilization.
- Re-work and failure.
- Activity variability.

Time and time again it has been possible to use computer tools, first to model and then improve industrial processes, speeding response, increasing throughput, and cutting costs.

At the same time, mimic diagrams of industrial processes have become commonplace, enabling operators to achieve better results from expensive plant and equipment, increasing productivity and safety and avoiding error.

An example of the power of such new techniques is SIMAN/CINEMA developed by the Systems Modeling Corporation in the USA. SIMAN is an event-driven simulation language used to describe elements in the process under study, such as machines, operators, storage, conveyors, cars, trains, and work pieces, specifically tailored to manufacturing and logistics applications. CINEMA is the animation tool used to create a visual image of the solution, providing a unique overview of the simulated system.

In developing a simulation, there are typically three project phases:

1 Identify the goal and specify the simulation to be undertaken.
2 Implement the modeling to create a validated and tested model.
3 Perform experiments with the model to explore different scenarios.

226

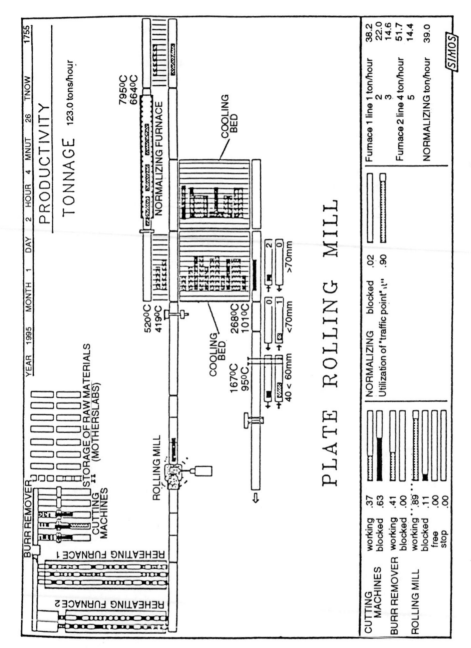

Figure A.13 Steel works layout design in plate rolling mill.

To illustrate such a simulation, take the example of simulating the performance of a steel rolling mill[2] shown in Figure A.13. The objective in this case was to evaluate the existing layout in terms of both throughput time and capacity utilization. The vision was to eliminate the buffers of plate stacks between critical processes, and link the processes closely together with new materials handling systems in the form of roller conveyors and cooling beds, with no buffers between the processes.

Simulation Goals

The goals of the simulation were to dimension the process capacities in terms of the number and capacity of cutting machines, determine the required lengths of furnaces and cooling beds and the material-handling capacities, while meeting process and product temperature constraints. Having solved this problem there was the additional objective of designing and testing various scheduling and planning strategies.

Simulation Model

The simulation model was built using SIMAN/CINEMA. Probability distributions describing the product and process data were estimated on the basis of production statistics from the last six months' production. To test the consequences of changes in the future product mix and process capacities, all parameters subject to change were built in as variables that could be changed in the simulation model.

---

[2] Examples of SIMAN/CINEMA have been taken from material supplied by SIMOS A/S, a member firm in Denmark of Coopers & Lybrand (International).

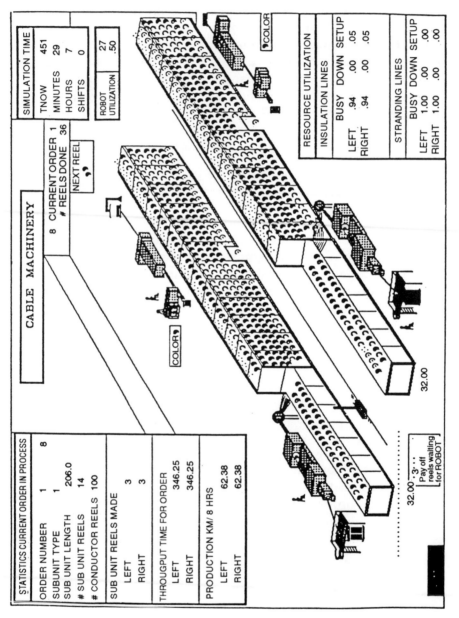

Figure A.14 Cable manufacturing.

Results of the Simulation

The simulation showed that the changed layout would result in a 10 percent reduction in overall capacity. However, by changing the planning and control strategies in use it was possible to increase achieved capacity utilization by 45 percent compared to the existing operation.

Figure A.14 is a second example of the use of SIMAN/CINEMA, this time in simulating the operation of a cable manufacturing facility. The aim here was to verify that a Just-In-Time concept could be applied to cable making, including reel and drum storage and retrieval, and the use of automatic guided vehicles and robotic transfer. The animation of the facility in the manner illustrated allowed Research and Development personnel to derive different performance operating statistics for comparison, and to choose between the different operating alternatives.

While simulation has found widespread use in the industrial environment, comparable computer systems have been developed to simulate processes in organizations such as banks and insurance companies, as well as in the back offices of industrial and commercial businesses. For this purpose the tools are somewhat different because it is necessary to represent operations such as documents, meetings, telexes, facsimiles, files, photocopying, data entry and calculation processes. An example of such a computer simulator is the SPARKS™ system developed for use in process simulation and analysis by Coopers & Lybrand (USA)[3]. The system runs on a high-powered workstation and creates models using iconic representations of the types shown in Figure A.15.

In the SPARKS system, entire processes are represented as combinations of the work elements so that a complete process mapping typically might consist of 100 or more icons to which performance statistics are carefully attached. By carrying out a dynamic simulation of the operation of a process it is possible to represent not only its average performance but also its variability, including the extent and costs of difficulties, exceptions,

---

[3] SPARKS™ is a registered trademark of Coopers & Lybrand (USA).

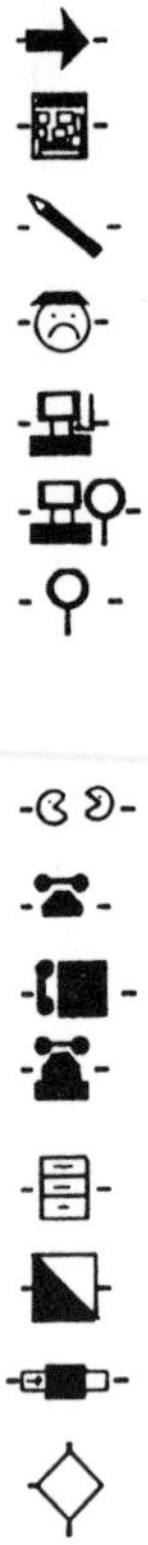

	TASK TYPE	NUMBER OF TASKS IN MODEL
➡	TRANSFER	# 8
🖩	CALCULATE	# 0
✎	DOCUMENT	# 82
☹	RESOLVE EXCEPTION	# 0
💻	ENTER DATA	# 6
💻	EXAMINE-DATA	# 0
♀	EXAMINE-DOCUMENT	# 7
	COMMUNICATE	# 41
C Ɔ	MEETING	# 22
☎	PHONE	# 18
☎	FAX	# 0
☎	TELEX	# 0
🗄	FILE	# 3
◣	RECONCILE	# 0
▣	PHOTOCOPY	# 1
◇	DECISION BRANCH	# 1
	TOTAL	

Figure A.15 *Iconic representation in SPARKS™ and typical task mix.*

and general non-conformance. An example of an elementary SPARKS representation is shown in Figure A.16. Figure A.17 shows how more aggregated representations can be generated if desired to construct a Quickmap of an entire process.

The power of SPARKS lies in its ability to create accurate representations and a wealth of operating performance statistics from which reengineering decisions can be made. Fully interactive on-line screen facilities supported by a state-of-the-art user interface make it a powerful supporter in achieving radical process change.

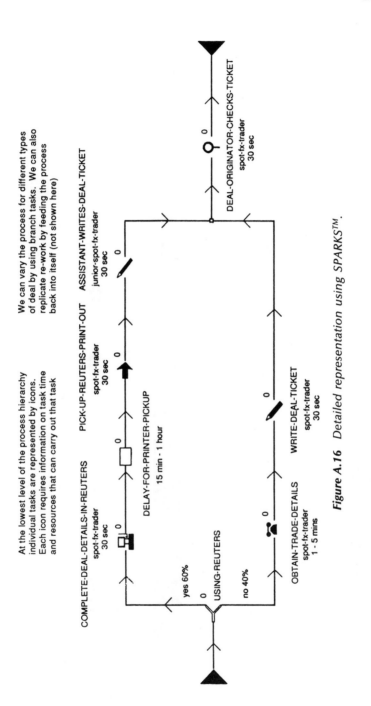

At the lowest level of the process hierarchy individual tasks are represented by icons. Each icon requires information on task time and resources that can carry out that task

We can vary the process for different types of deal by using branch tasks. We can also replicate re-work by feeding the process back into itself (not shown here)

COMPLETE-DEAL-DETAILS-IN-REUTERS
spot-fx-trader
30 sec

PICK-UP-REUTERS-PRINT-OUT
spot-fx-trader
30 sec

ASSISTANT-WRITES-DEAL-TICKET
junior-spot-fx-trader
30 sec

DEAL-ORIGINATOR-CHECKS-TICKET
spot-fx-trader
30 sec

DELAY-FOR-PRINTER-PICKUP
15 min - 1 hour

WRITE-DEAL-TICKET
spot-fx-trader
30 sec

OBTAIN-TRADE-DETAILS
spot-fx-trader
1 - 5 mins

USING-REUTERS

yes 60%

no 40%

Figure A.16 Detailed representation using SPARKS™.

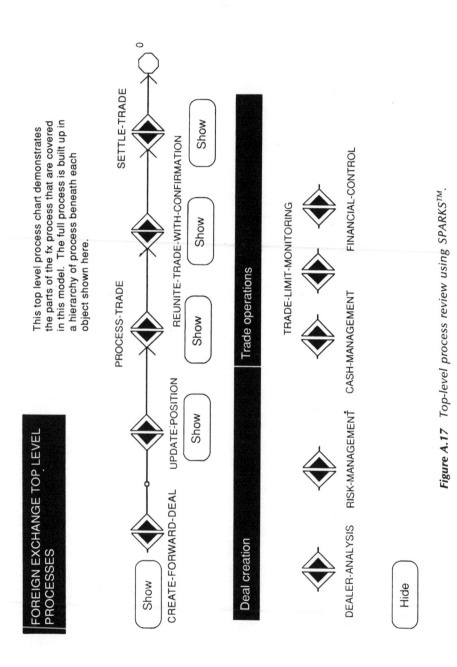

FOREIGN EXCHANGE TOP LEVEL PROCESSES

This top level process chart demonstrates the parts of the fx process that are covered in this model. The full process is built up in a hierarchy of process beneath each object shown here.

CREATE-FORWARD-DEAL

UPDATE-POSITION

PROCESS-TRADE

REUNITE-TRADE-WITH-CONFIRMATION

SETTLE-TRADE

Show

Show

Show

Show

Show

Deal creation

Trade operations

DEALER-ANALYSIS

RISK-MANAGEMENT

CASH-MANAGEMENT

TRADE-LIMIT-MONITORING

FINANCIAL-CONTROL

Hide

Figure A.17 Top-level process review using SPARKS™.

PITFALLS OF PROCESS MAPPING AND DATA MODELING

In the context of Business Process Reengineering, process mapping plays an essential part in challenging existing processes by helping to pose a variety of critical questions:

- Is the complexity necessary?
- Are simplifications possible?
- Are there too many interdepartmental transfers?
- Are people empowered to fulfill their function?
- Is the process effective?
- Is work carried out efficiently?
- Are costs appropriate?
- Is there significant variability in load?
- What drives process cost?
- How is quality assured?

There are dangers, however, in indiscriminate use. There is often a tendency to take too long and spend too much money on analysis at the expense of applying resources to the creation of new and better processes supported by a vigorous program of change. It is for this reason that the methods advocated for use by the authors usually feature the ability to achieve a step-wise decomposition of processes into subprocesses and their constituent underlying activities. This is not, however, to detract from the value of information.

Scientific methods of process analysis from the Taylorism of the 1880s to the present day depend crucially on the gathering of facts followed by the use of an appropriate means of analysis. On many occasions, particularly in industrial process analysis, the sifting of vast amounts of data is an essential part of the investigation and cannot be overlooked.

The danger most to be avoided is that of "paralysis by analysis," in which no progress is made toward defining new ways of working because what was supposed to be a means to an end—the analysis of data—becomes an end in itself, and begins totally to preoccupy Business Process Reengineering project teams.

Process mapping of existing processes should be allowed to proceed no further than necessary to allow the formation of a vision of a new process. It is to the new process that attention should be directed as soon as possible.

In seeking to achieve BreakPoints in performance in the market it is likely that time needs to be spent on the major process issues, such as "is the process really needed at all?" rather than in making minor modifications to the minutiae of individual worksteps which, more often than not, will find their treatment in the on-going evolutionary change inherent in continuous improvement programs.

Index

Index compiled by Indexing Specialists, Hove, East Sussex, UK

Compensation ~~operating~~ credit

100% participation

Calendar

define – what are processes
       how to evaluates/map

process redesign
related systems. needing redesign/parking lots
    ie HR, comp, staffing

formal change management
            need mission/objectives
Goals what do we want pg 57
        o

white paper – Getting on the same
page / with a bibliography
recommendations / call to action

(need
    marketing Diversity

stmts – questions
Sample process